ISIS's Use of
Sexual Violence in Iraq

Christel Ghandour

ISIS's Use of Sexual Violence in Iraq

Christel Ghandour

St. James's Studies in World Affairs

Academica Press
Washington – London

Library of Congress Cataloging-in-Publication Data

Names: Ghandour, Christel, author.
Title: ISIS's use of sexual violence in Iraq / Christel Ghandour.
Description: Washington, DC : Academica Press, 2019. | Includes
bibliographical references.
Identifiers: LCCN 2018055610 | ISBN 9781680534719 (hardcover : alk.
paper)
| ISBN 9781680534948 (pbk. : alk. paper)
Subjects: LCSH: Yezidi women--Violence against--Iraq. | Women--
Violence
against--Iraq. | Sex crimes--Iraq. | Rape--Iraq. | Women and war--Iraq. |
IS (Organization)
Classification: LCC DS70.8.Y49 G53 2019 | DDC 956.7044/3--dc23
LC record available at https://lccn.loc.gov/2018055610

Contents

Acknowledgments

This book is dedicated to every woman who has suffered from gender-based violence. I am grateful to the Yezidi women I have met in Iraq who did not allow me to feel that they were victims, but rather survivors who had fought the biggest battle of their lives. I would like to thank my supervisor, Dr. Jelle van Buuren, for being supportive during a very critical time while I was writing the thesis on which this book is based. He gave me the freedom and patience that I needed in order to undertake such a sensitive and complex topic. I would like to thank my family for pushing me to my limits and for constantly inspiring me to carry on. Last but not least, I would like to thank my friends, who were able to tolerate the panic and sometimes the sadness while I was writing.

Chapter 1:
Introduction

"Rape has been used throughout history as a weapon of war. I never thought I would have something in common with women in Rwanda—before all this, I didn't know that a country called Rwanda existed—and now I am linked to them in the worst possible way, as a victim of a war crime that is so hard to talk about that no one in the world was prosecuted for committing it until just sixteen years before ISIS came to Sinjar."[1] ~ Nadia Murad, Yezidi Survivor

In the summer of 2014, the Islamic State of Iraq and the Levant (ISIL), more commonly identified as the Islamic State in Iraq and Syria (ISIS), attacked the Yezidi villages surrounding the Mount Sinjar region of Northwestern Iraq. The area was home to at least 400,000 Yezidis. In a matter of hours, ISIS swept through the villages and systematically separated the men from the women and children. The men were executed, young boys were assessed to determine if they had or had not reached puberty so that ISIS could either train them as child soldiers or, if they were too old, execute them along with the adult males. Women were sorted according to their marital status, aesthetic appeal, and age

---

[1] Murad, Nadia, and Jenna Krajeski. "Chapter 5." *The Last Girl: My Story of Captivity, and My Fight against the Islamic State.* 1st ed. New York: Tim Duggan, 2017. 46-55. Print.

and sold as sex slaves. Despite the international community's expressions of shock, this was not the first time this has happened, and the methods used for separation were not entirely unique.

1.1 The research

1.1.1 Problem statement

Sexual violence in conflict is defined by the United Nations as "rape, sexual slavery, forced prostitution, forced pregnancy, forced abortion, enforced sterilization, forced marriage, [sexual trafficking] and any other form of sexual violence of comparable gravity perpetrated against women, men, girls or boys that is directly or indirectly linked to a conflict."[2] Even though such sexually related crimes are of unspeakable horror, their effects are far more insidious. For instance, sexual violence in conflict has caused great trauma to communities by "displacing civilians from strategic areas, eliciting operational intelligence, and forcing conversions through marriage."[3] This, in turn, ultimately leads to the complete annihilation of ethnic minorities within those communities, and in cases in which survivors tend not to return to their homes. On another note, sexual violence in conflict is not a phenomenon that is necessarily always directly related to male sexual needs in time of war.

---

[2] Office of the Special Representative of the Secretary-general on Sexual Violence in Conflict. *Report of the Secretary-General on Conflict-Related Sexual Violence.* Rep. no. 249. United Nations, 15 Apr. 2017. Web. 25 July 2018. <http://www.un.org/en/events/elimination-of-sexual-violence-in-conflict/pdf/1494280398.pdf>.

[3] Office of the Special Representative of the Secretary-general on Sexual Violence in Conflict. *Report of the Secretary-General on Conflict-Related Sexual Violence.* Rep. no. 249. United Nations, 15 Apr. 2017. Web. 25 July 2018. <http://www.un.org/en/events/elimination-of-sexual-violence-in-conflict/pdf/1494280398.pdf>.

In some instances, it can be a calculated and institutionalized means of reaching one's strategic goals. It can be used to "generate revenue, as part of the shadow economy of conflict and terrorism, through sex trafficking, sexual slavery, enforced prostitution and the extortion of ransoms from desperate families,"[4] for example. In such cases, captured women and girls are considered "wages of war" as they are gifted to fighters as a means of compensation. Survivors of sexual violence in conflict face ostracism from their communities and families as they are thought to have brought shame to their family names. As a result, survivors usually resort to moving and living elsewhere, being displaced entirely or, in more drastic cases, to illicit means of living. As such, sexual violence in conflict is a grave violation of human rights. Its effects are severe, chronic, and perpetual, especially if not managed and addressed in a suitable manner.

1.1.2 Research Aims & Objectives

This book explores how and why ISIS has organized and used sexual violence against Yezidi women in Iraq. Key conceptual and theoretical frameworks on sexual violence will be used throughout the book as means of understanding how current approaches towards sexual violence are shaped. In essence, this book aims to answer the question: How can ISIS's use of sexual violence against the Yezidi women in Iraq be explained? In order to answer the main research question, three main

---

[4] Office of the Special Representative of the Secretary-general on Sexual Violence in Conflict. *Report of the Secretary-General on Conflict-Related Sexual Violence.* Rep. no. 249. United Nations, 15 Apr. 2017. Web. 25 July 2018. <http://www.un.org/en/events/elimination-of-sexual-violence-in-conflict/pdf/1494280398.pdf>.

theories that explain sexual violence will be tested against the findings of the single case study.

ISIS's use of sexual violence against the Yezidi women, in particular, is rather puzzling because when Yezidi women were captured, they tended to be used as sex slaves, an approach, their predecessors, al-Qaeda in Iraq, (AQI) and similar jihadi groups had not previously used.

1.1.3 Academic relevance

This book intends to provide an understanding on how sexual violence is used as a deliberate strategy of war and conflict. One issue that arises from studying sexual violence during times of conflict is that no two instances of such acts are necessarily the same. In essence, because the circumstances and reasoning behind instances of sexual violence during conflict is contextual there, will always be a need for and significance in researching such an issue. In order to capture and understand sexual violence in conflict, this investigation will apply three main theories to this single case study. The three main theories are 1) evolution theory by Craig Palmer and Randy Thornhill, 2) feminist theory based on Susan Brownmiller's work, and 3) Strategic Rape concept. Applying these theories to this single case study will highlight their limitations yet also highlight additional elements to explain sexual violence in conflict. Moreover, although the use of sexual violence in conflict is not new, information on the topic is relatively rare due to the sensitivity and complexity of the topic.

1.1.4 Societal relevance

Understanding why ISIS has utilized this type of violence helps to demystify the group and explains their behavior, which one hopes may help prevent any future acts of sexual violence. This book's further significance lies in how the case of the Yezidi women has yet to be fully examined in detail. Using the case of the Yezidi women, it hopes to produce an understanding of sexual violence in conflict that garners inspiration and ideas taken from a multidisciplinary approach towards crisis management, which highlights the human security element.

1.2 Organization of the Book

The second chapter reviews the extant literature, including various theories and concepts that explain sexual violence in conflict, including the evolution theory, feminist theory, and strategic rape concept used herein as analytical tools. This chapter is crucial for laying a conceptual and theoretical foundation for this single-case study. The third chapter presents the background of both ISIS and the Yezidi community in order to provide context for the reader. This chapter will help the reader see the big picture. The fourth chapter presents the methodology used in this research. The research is designed as a single-case study. The triangulation of qualitative methods consists of semi-structured, informal, and open-ended interviews, and fieldwork. The aim of this chapter is to provide a clear understanding and justification for how the information was provided and why it was needed to fulfill this investigation. The chapter will also present the limitations, security considerations, and ethical dilemmas that were encountered while gathering information. The fifth chapter will present the findings of the desk research and interviews in a narrative structure. This will provide a sort of story that depicts what happened to the survivors through the author's lens. The sixth chapter will present an analysis of the findings by bridging the theoretical and the practical. The findings will be analyzed through the testing of multiple theories and concepts in order to explore which explanation is the most applicable to this case study. The book concludes with chapter seven, which summarizes the main conclusions and presents the author's reflections and recommendations for future research.

Chapter 2:
Body of Knowledge

2.1 Overview of the Construct of Sexual Violence

This chapter will provide a brief definition of the main terms and concepts and then discuss the three main theoretical approaches and conceptualizations of sexual violence in conflict. These include Evolution Theory, Feminist Theory, and Strategic Rape Concept. Evolution Theory, in essence, conceptualizes sexual desire as a common motivation for rape, tracing such desires back to the evolution of men's sexual psychology.[5] On the other hand, Feminist Theory iterates the power dimension of sexual violence.[6] This research will manly focus on the work of Susan Brownmiller, the leading classical feminist theorist of wartime sexual violence. Most scholars, however, tend to adopt the strategic rape concept as the leading theory to explore sexual violence in conflict. This concept emphasizes the difference between strategic and

---

[5] Thornhill, Randy, and Craig T. Palmer. "Rape and Evolutionary Theory." *A Natural History of Rape: Biological Bases of Sexual Coercion.* Cambridge, MA: MIT, 2000. 1-30. Print.
[6] Brownmiller, Susan. "War." *Against Our Will: Men, Women and Rape.* New York: Ballantine, 1993. 31-113. Print.

non-strategic rape in time of war and conflict.[7] The work of Anne Llewellyn Barstow on the strategic rape concept, elaborated in her book *War's Dirty Secret: Rape, Prostitution, and Other Crimes Against Women,*[8] will be reviewed in this book, as her work is a compilation of various cases which support her approach.

In addition to reviewing the three dominant theories on sexual violence, other concepts will be briefly presented towards the end of the chapter. These additional concepts include the scholarship of Elizabeth Jean Wood, which includes her work on variation[9] and multiple perpetrator rape during war;[10] a brief look into religious ideology in reference to ISIS's use of sexual violence; and the geostrategic element of the use of sexual violence in conflict.

2.2 Terms and Definitions

In order to avoid confusion over the definition of the terms used in this thesis, it is paramount to conceptualize and define the terms that will be used. The first term that will be defined is "sexual violence in conflict." Although there are several definitions, the most recent, formulated by the United Nations (UN) in 2017, will be utilized in this

---

[7] Barstow, Anne Llewellyn. "Introduction." *War's Dirty Secret: Rape, Prostitution, and Other Crimes against Women.* Ed. Anne Llewellyn. Barstow. Cleveland, OH: Pilgrim, 2000. 1-10. Print.

[8] Barstow, Anne Llewellyn. "Introduction." *War's Dirty Secret: Rape, Prostitution, and Other Crimes against Women.* Ed. Anne Llewellyn. Barstow. Cleveland, OH: Pilgrim, 2000. 1-10. Print.

[9] Wood, Elisabeth Jean. "Variation in Sexual Violence during War." *Politics & Society* 34.3 (2006): 307-41. *Politics & Society.* Sage Publications, Sept. 2006. Web. 25 Mar. 2017.

[10] Wood, Elisabeth Jean. "Multiple Perpetrator Rape during War." *Handbook on the Study of Multiple Perpetrator Rape: A Multidisciplinary Response to an International Problem.* Ed. Miranda A. H. Horvath and Jessica Woodhams. London: Routledge, Taylor & Francis, 2013. 132-59. Print.

book. According to this definition, "sexual violence in conflict" refers to "rape, sexual slavery, forced prostitution, forced pregnancy, forced abortion, enforced sterilization, forced marriage, [sexual trafficking] and any other form of sexual violence of comparable gravity perpetrated against women, men, girls or boys that is directly or indirectly linked to a conflict."[11] This definition was presented in the report by the Secretary General's office pursuant to Security Council Resolution 2106 (2013), which requested that the Secretary General monitor the implementation of Resolutions 1820 (2008), 1888 (2009), and 1960 (2010).[12] This definition was chosen because previous definitions, including those of the International Criminal Tribunal for Rwanda (ICTR) and the International Criminal Tribunal for Yugoslavia (ICTY), both failed to mention sexual slavery, which is an important element for this case study.

Elizabeth Jean Wood provided a pragmatic definition of sexual slavery by stating "in some conflicts, sexual violence takes the form of sexual slavery, whereby women are abducted to serve as servants and sexual partners of combatants for an extended period; in others, it takes the form of torture in detention."[13] The slavery convention define slavery but does not explicitly define sexual slavery; therefore, Wood's definition of sexual slavery will be applied in this book.

---

[11] Office of the Special Representative of the Secretary-general on Sexual Violence in Conflict. *Report of the Secretary-General on Conflict-Related Sexual Violence*. Rep. no. 249. United Nations, 15 Apr. 2017. Web.

[12] Office of the Special Representative of the Secretary-general on Sexual Violence in Conflict. *Report of the Secretary-General on Conflict-Related Sexual Violence*. Rep. no. 249. United Nations, 15 Apr. 2017. Web.

[13] Wood, Elisabeth Jean. "Variation in Sexual Violence during War." *Politics & Society* 34.3 (2006): 307-41. *Politics & Society*. Sage Publications, Sept. 2006. Web. 25 Mar. 2017.

In this book, the "Islamic State" will be referred to as the colloquial "ISIS" employed in the title rather than the more formal designation "Islamic State in Iraq and the Levant" (ISIL). ISIS's evolution started in 2000. Between 2000 and 2009, it was known as the Musab al-Zarqawi Network and mainly consisted of a small group of Levantine Islamists who crossed paths in their respective countries or in Afghanistan.[14] This small group followed Zarqawi to Iraq in 2003 and called themselves Jamiat Al-Tawhid wa al-Jihad (the group of Monotheism and Jihad).[15] In 2004, the group was then renamed Tanzim al–Qaedat al-Jihad fi Bilad al-Rafidain (Organization of the Jihad base in the Land of the Two Rivers), after joining Al Qaeda, which led to the simpler name "Al Qaeda in Iraq," or AQI.[16] In 2006, AQI turned into Majlis Shura al-Mujahidin fi al-Iraq (the mujahidin council MSC) due to its heightened violence, which led the group to gather more like-minded people.[17] A few years later, Abu Omar al-Baghdadi, the MSC leader, formed al-Dawla al-islamiyya fi al-Iraq (the Islamic State in Iraq, or ISI).[18] In 2013 the group in turn became Sawlat al-Islam fi al-Iraq wa Bilad al-Sham (the Islamic state of Iraq and Syria-ISIS), after Abu

---

[14] Hashim, Ahmed S. "Understanding the Islamic State." *The Caliphate at War: The Ideological, Organisational and Military Innovations of Islamic State.* London: Hurst, 2016. 3-16. Print.

[15] Hashim, Ahmed S. "Understanding the Islamic State." *The Caliphate at War: The Ideological, Organisational and Military Innovations of Islamic State.* London: Hurst, 2016. 3-16. Print.

[16] Hashim, Ahmed S. "Understanding the Islamic State." *The Caliphate at War: The Ideological, Organisational and Military Innovations of Islamic State.* London: Hurst, 2016. 3-16. Print.

[17] Hashim, Ahmed S. "Understanding the Islamic State." *The Caliphate at War: The Ideological, Organisational and Military Innovations of Islamic State.* London: Hurst, 2016. 3-16. Print.

[18] Hashim, Ahmed S. "Understanding the Islamic State." *The Caliphate at War: The Ideological, Organisational and Military Innovations of Islamic State.* London: Hurst, 2016. 3-16. Print.

Omar's successor, Abu Bakr al-Baghdadi, extended operations into Syria.[19] The United States government initially preferred to call the group the Islamic State of Iraq and the Levant (ISIL),[20] which made sense since its ideology reflects its goal of interfering in the Levant, broadly defined beyond official national boundaries. Moreover, it also reflects their territorial identity. Although the group began referring to itself as the Islamic State (IS) after declaring a new "Caliphate" in June 2014, it proved difficult to place all the Muslims in the world under that banner so this designation became problematic.

2.3 Evolution Theory

Evolution Theory, pioneered by Charles Darwin and other nineteenth-century naturalists, is "the process by which organisms change over time as a result of changes in heritable physical behavioral traits. Changes that allow an organism to better adapt to its environment will help it survive and have more offspring."[21] The theory is commonly associated with Herbert Spencer's phrase "survival of the fittest" because it focuses on an organism's capacity to survive and reproduce. The repetitive use of this "biological" explanation of rape in both academic and social circles is one of the reasons why it is important to present and assess this approach.

---

[19] Hashim, Ahmed S. "Understanding the Islamic State." *The Caliphate at War: The Ideological, Organisational and Military Innovations of Islamic State.* London: Hurst, 2016. 3-16. Print.
[20] Hashim, Ahmed S. "Understanding the Islamic State." *The Caliphate at War: The Ideological, Organisational and Military Innovations of Islamic State.* London: Hurst, 2016. 3-16. Print.
[21] Than, Ker. "What Is Darwin's Theory of Evolution?" *LiveScience.* Purch, 13 May 2015. Web. 03 Dec. 2017.

Randy Thornhill and Craig Palmer apply Evolution Theory to rape in their book, *A Natural History of Rape*. They define rape as "copulation resisted to the last of the victim's ability unless such resistance would probably result in death or serious injury to the victim or in death or injury to individuals the victim commonly protects."[22] Thornhill and Palmer present the ultimate reason for the occurrence of rape: that "sexual desire is a common motivation for human rape and that this desire ultimately traces back to men's evolved sexual psychology."[23] According to Evolution Theory, men are naturally more eager than women to pursue mating, which consequently triggers females to select males who compete for access to the female.[24] Therefore, since selection by the female is the only way to mate, males choose to bypass this selection process and rape the female for fear of not being chosen, thus enhancing reproductive success.[25] Another evolutionary reason for males to choose rape could result from females preferring particular traits in their mates. This will likely trigger a male with undesirable traits to circumvent a female's preference and resort to rape.[26] According to Evolution Theory, if a woman was not particularly selective and would

---

[22] Thornhill, Randy, and Craig T. Palmer. "Rape and Evolutionary Theory." *A Natural History of Rape: Biological Bases of Sexual Coercion*. Cambridge, MA: MIT, 2000. 1-30. Print.

[23] Gottschall, Jonathan. "Explaining Wartime Rape." *The Journal of Sex Research* 41.2 (2004): 129-36. *JSTOR*. Web. 21 Apr. 2017.

[24] Thornhill, Randy, and Craig T. Palmer. "Why Do Men Rape?" *A Natural History of Rape: Biological Bases of Sexual Coercion*. Cambridge, MA: MIT, 2000. 53-84. Print.

[25] Thornhill, Randy, and Craig T. Palmer. "Why Do Men Rape?" *A Natural History of Rape: Biological Bases of Sexual Coercion*. Cambridge, MA: MIT, 2000. 53-84. Print.

[26] Thornhill, Randy, and Craig T. Palmer. "Why Do Men Rape?" *A Natural History of Rape: Biological Bases of Sexual Coercion*. Cambridge, MA: MIT, 2000. 53-84. Print.

agree to mate regardless of her preferences, rape could be avoided. Or, if a male were only attracted to a certain type of female, then rape also could have been avoided by other types. Such an argument, however, depends on natural selection behaving exclusively in the aforementioned manner.[27] This also implies that the proximate cause is male and female sexuality, and that the persistence of an instinct to rape that is inherited.

The logic behind Thornhill's and Palmer's claim that the instinct to rape is ultimately due to male genetic inheritance is based on the two levels of causation. The two causations are proximate and ultimate. Proximate causations are immediate causes, those that operate over a short period of time, usually including "genes, hormones, physiological structures (including brain mechanisms), and environmental stimuli (including environmental experiences that affect learning)."[28] In other words, proximate causation stresses the "how" while on the other hand ultimate causation stresses the "why." Ultimate causation explains why there are proximate causations, thus making both types of causation complementary only in cases in which proximate causation is adequately explained by the ultimate cause. The authors are not concerned with why a male commits rape but rather with *how* he commits rape, taking social and environmental contexts as the cause of his behavior. They stress biological traits as the main causes: if one wants to understand the ultimate cause of rape, one must first understand how natural selection causes adaptation. According to Thornhill and Palmer, adaptations are

---

[27] Thornhill, Randy, and Craig T. Palmer. "Why Do Men Rape?" *A Natural History of Rape: Biological Bases of Sexual Coercion.* Cambridge, MA: MIT, 2000. 53-84. Print.

[28] Thornhill, Randy, and Craig T. Palmer. "Rape and Evolutionary Theory." *A Natural History of Rape: Biological Bases of Sexual Coercion.* Cambridge, MA: MIT, 2000. 1-30. Print.

the favorable behavioral and physiological traits manifested because they were favorable and advanced from the past through natural selection.[29] As the authors are concerned with only the ultimate cause of rape, this suggests that all other contexts of causation are ignored. Importantly for this study, according to Thornhill and Palmer's argument, the context of war cannot be used to explain rape in time of conflict.

Although Thornhill and Palmer use natural selection as their premise to explain the cause of rape, this creates a debate between the authors and evolutionary theorists: whether rape is an adaptation that resulted from natural selection or whether it is a byproduct of other adaptations. The mere existence of such a debate in this context implies that explaining rape through the lens of Evolution Theory begs the question of whether men commit rape for biological reasons. Nevertheless, they are incapable of distinguishing whether or not rape is an adaptation per se. On another note, Evolution Theory suggests that the ultimate "benefit" of rape is to facilitate reproduction. Does such a claim imply that all males who rape want on some level to reproduce? If the "benefit" or reproductive success of rape is higher than the cost or punishment of death, then how does this explain the higher frequency of rape during conflict, especially rape of elderly women and prepubescent girls who are clearly incapable of reproduction?

---

[29] Thornhill, Randy, and Craig T. Palmer. "Rape and Evolutionary Theory." *A Natural History of Rape: Biological Bases of Sexual Coercion*. Cambridge, MA: MIT, 2000. 1-30. Print.

2.4 Feminist Theory

According to a succinct definition, "Feminist theory explores both inequality in gender and the constitution of gender."[30] Feminist Theory is in essence the theoretical extension of feminism, which includes numerous themes, including oppression, phenomenology, and sexual objectification.[31] While some feminist theorists focus on gender inequality and how it is observed in various social institutions, others focus on how certain practices are labeled as "feminine" or "masculine" and how gender is perceived in the social context.[32] Thus, feminist theory aims to account for the subordination of women in order to find the root causes of women's oppression.

The feminist school of thought is integral to understanding sexual violence in conflict, and feminists were among the first scholars to assess and document mass rape in conflict.[33] One of the main feminist pioneers, Susan Brownmiller, related feminist theory to sexual violence in her 1975 book *Against Our Will*. Using a historical analysis of sexual violence and rape in conflict, Brownmiller explained why such an issue has not been chronicled enough despite its frequent occurrence in conflict. She stated that women were prohibited from exploring male sexuality in on order "to discover the truth and meaning in [their] own

---

[30] Carlson, Jennifer, and Raka Ray. "Feminist Theory." *Oxford Bibliographies*. Oxford, 20 Nov. 2011. Web. 04 Dec. 2017.

[31] Butler, Judith. "Performative Acts and Gender Constitution: An Essay in Phenomenology and Feminist Theory." *Theatre Journal* 40.4 (1988): 519-31. *JSTOR [JSTOR]*. Web. 4 Dec. 2017.

[32] Carlson, Jennifer, and Raka Ray. "Feminist Theory." *Oxford Bibliographies*. Oxford, 20 Nov. 2011. Web. 04 Dec. 2017.

[33] Gottschall, Jonathan. "Explaining Wartime Rape." *The Journal of Sex Research* 41.2 (2004): 129-36. *JSTOR*. Web. 21 Apr. 2017.

victimization."[34] Brownmiller maintained that in order to understand the current rape culture one must first understand the history of rape. She stressed the importance of historical analysis due to the interpretation of many male scholars, specifically those who favor Evolution Theory, who have regarded sexual violence and rape as a byproduct of "human nature."[35] Theorists such as Freud, Marx, Engels, and Wilhelm Reich tended to ignore rape and regarded it as a secondary pain to a man's search for labor.[36] Accordingly, Evolution Theory contradicts feminist theory. While the former provides an evolution-based theory that suggests that rape results from an evolutionary urge (lust and the aim to procreate), the latter suggests that it has nothing to do with biology (lust) but rather a male's power over the female, thus desexualizing the act. Moreover, Evolution Theory, as previously mentioned, ignores social contexts that play a role in rape, while feminist theory stresses context to prove how environment and ideology play a role in rape.[37]

Feminist Theory clearly argues that rape in conflict has nothing to do with sexual desire, but rather with misogyny.[38] Conflict arguably provides men with an ideal platform in which to exert their dominance

---

[34] Brownmiller, Susan. "The Mass Psychology of Rape: An Introduction." *Against Our Will: Men, Women and Rape*. New York: Ballantine, 1993. 11-15. Print.

[35] Gottschall, Jonathan. "Explaining Wartime Rape." *The Journal of Sex Research* 41.2 (2004): 129-36. *JSTOR*. Web. 21 Apr. 2017.

[36] Brownmiller, Susan. "The Mass Psychology of Rape: An Introduction." *Against Our Will: Men, Women and Rape*. New York: Ballantine, 1993. 11-15. Print.

[37] Wood, Elisabeth Jean. "Variation in Sexual Violence during War." *Politics & Society* 34.3 (2006): 307-41. *Politics & Society*. Sage Publications, Sept. 2006. Web. 25 Mar. 2017.

[38] Brownmiller, Susan. "The Mass Psychology of Rape: An Introduction." *Against Our Will: Men, Women and Rape*. New York: Ballantine, 1993. 11-15. Print.

over women.[39] Accordingly, feminist theorists largely hold the opinion that acts of sexual violence are almost always a by-product of conflict. This is due to men's power struggle with women, thus when given the opportunity, some may choose to rape women.[40] Such a perspective asserts that regardless of culture, religion, or social traits, sexual violence in conflict is widespread and not due to a man's human nature.[41]

According to Feminist Theory, males who rape during conflict are argued to be the "victors" for two reasons.[42] First, women are equated with property and can thus end up being considered compensation, or spoils of war, like land and cattle. Rape, in this sense, is seen as the act of the conqueror and an indicator of victory in conflict.[43] During medieval times, one of the main motives for common foot soldiers to go to war was the opportunity to rape and loot since monetary compensation by their leaders was irregular at best.[44]/[45] Second, and more psychological, rape in war helped secure masculinity and male dominance over the women of the defeated side.[46] Hence, raping a woman on the defeated

---

[39] Brownmiller, Susan. "The Mass Psychology of Rape: An Introduction." *Against Our Will: Men, Women and Rape.* New York: Ballantine, 1993. 11-15. Print.

[40] Gottschall, Jonathan. "Explaining Wartime Rape." *The Journal of Sex Research* 41.2 (2004): 129-36. *JSTOR.* Web. 21 Apr. 2017.

[41] Gottschall, Jonathan. "Explaining Wartime Rape." *The Journal of Sex Research* 41.2 (2004): 129-36. *JSTOR.* Web. 21 Apr. 2017.

[42] Brownmiller, Susan. "War." *Against Our Will: Men, Women and Rape.* New York: Ballantine, 1993. 31-113. Print.

[43] Brownmiller, Susan. "War." *Against Our Will: Men, Women and Rape.* New York: Ballantine, 1993. 31-113. Print.

[44] Brownmiller, Susan. "War." *Against Our Will: Men, Women and Rape.* New York: Ballantine, 1993. 31-113. Print.

[45] This was evident when the "Byzantine emperor Alexius extolled the beauty of Greek women in his appeals for recruits for the First Crusade.

[46] Brownmiller, Susan. "War." *Against Our Will: Men, Women and Rape.* New York: Ballantine, 1993. 31-113. Print.

side was both a measure of success for the victors and massive humiliation of the defeated, a "sexual coup de grace."[47] This implies that having the defeated side's women violated is a blow to the masculinity and honor of their men, who failed to protect them. As such, "rape by conquering soldier destroys all remaining illusions of power and property for men at the defeated side." [48] An even greater effect was to force the men of the family watch their women being raped.[49] Moreover, rape acted as a means of deliberate intimidation and demoralization as it is not only an attack on the women but also the men of the defeated society.[50]

Ideology in conflict can also constitute a motive for rape.[51] One example of this is that of the rape of the Huguenot, or Protestant, women in France by Catholic soldiers during the Wars of Religions in the 1500s. Women were separated from their husbands, brutally raped, humiliated in the streets, and then taken to church to atone and beg for forgiveness for forsaking the Catholic faith.[52]

The concept of anonymity can also be applied to understanding sexual violence in conflict. This is evident in the early stages of the Vietnam Conflict. The South Vietnamese army participated in rape,

---

[47] Brownmiller, Susan. "War." *Against Our Will: Men, Women and Rape*. New York: Ballantine, 1993. 31-113. Print.
[48] Brownmiller, Susan. "War." *Against Our Will: Men, Women and Rape*. New York: Ballantine, 1993. 31-113. Print.
[49] Brownmiller, Susan. "War." *Against Our Will: Men, Women and Rape*. New York: Ballantine, 1993. 31-113. Print.
[50] Brownmiller, Susan. "War." *Against Our Will: Men, Women and Rape*. New York: Ballantine, 1993. 31-113. Print.
[51] Brownmiller, Susan. "War." *Against Our Will: Men, Women and Rape*. New York: Ballantine, 1993. 31-113. Print.
[52] Brownmiller, Susan. "War." *Against Our Will: Men, Women and Rape*. New York: Ballantine, 1993. 31-113. Print.

though very little, at the beginning of the conflict.[53] Their reluctance arose from the possibility that potential victims could be women from well-connected families or women who were related to them.[54] However, when the South Vietnamese soldiers invaded Cambodia, a foreign country, in 1970 they were much less reluctant to commit rape and other crimes.[55] It was easier for them to dehumanize women with whom they had neither familiarity nor blood relation.[56]

As previously mentioned, sexual violence comes in various forms, which of which is sexual slavery.[57] Sexual slavery occurs when "women are abducted to serve as servants and sexual partners of combatants for extended periods."[58] Brownmiller argues that sexual slavery "was an institutional crime, part and parcel of the white man's subjugation of a people for economic and psychological gain."[59] Brownmiller makes an instructive contrast between sexual violence that happened during the Indian Wars, American campaigns against Native Americans, and the sexual violence that happened during slavery in the American South. During the Indian Wars, sexual violence was retaliatory

---

[53] Brownmiller, Susan. "War." *Against Our Will: Men, Women and Rape*. New York: Ballantine, 1993. 31-113. Print.
[54] Brownmiller, Susan. "War." *Against Our Will: Men, Women and Rape*. New York: Ballantine, 1993. 31-113. Print.
[55] Brownmiller, Susan. "War." *Against Our Will: Men, Women and Rape*. New York: Ballantine, 1993. 31-113. Print.
[56] Brownmiller, Susan. "War." *Against Our Will: Men, Women and Rape*. New York: Ballantine, 1993. 31-113. Print.
[57] Wood, Elisabeth Jean. "Variation in Sexual Violence during War." *Politics & Society* 34.3 (2006): 307-41. *Politics & Society*. Sage Publications, Sept. 2006. Web. 25 Mar. 2017.
[58] Wood, Elisabeth Jean. "Variation in Sexual Violence during War." *Politics & Society* 34.3 (2006): 307-41. *Politics & Society*. Sage Publications, Sept. 2006. Web. 25 Mar. 2017.
[59] Brownmiller, Susan. "Two Studies in American History." *Against Our Will: Men, Women and Rape*. New York: Ballantine, 1993. 140-73. Print.

in nature, in that men were using acts of sexual violence as a means of revenge. On the other hand, sexual violence in American slave states took form as part of the patriarchal institution, in which slave owning white males held legal dominance over black females.[60] Brownmiller further stresses the concept of economic and psychological gain when referring to how slave owners had quick and direct access to non-consensual sex with female slaves. Sexual slavery was not considered a crime at the time since the slaveholders wrote the laws and slaves were legal property.[61]

Michel Foucault, another leading figure identified with the feminist school of thought, approached rape by first desexualizing it.[62] In other words, he took out the sex from rape and treated it purely as an act of violence.[63] This is evident from his claim that "sexuality can in no circumstance be the object of punishment. And when one punished rape one should be punishing physical violence and nothing but that."[64] Although not all feminist intellectuals agreed with this statement, it did resonate with some, such as Laura Hengehold.[65] She argues that an assault by a penis is no different from assault by any other human body part, and that physical assault is thus essentially the same as sexual

---

[60] Brownmiller, Susan. "Two Studies in American History." *Against Our Will: Men, Women and Rape.* New York: Ballantine, 1993. 140-73. Print.

[61] Brownmiller, Susan. "Two Studies in American History." *Against Our Will: Men, Women and Rape.* New York: Ballantine, 1993. 140-73. Print.

[62] Henderson, Holly. "Feminism, Foucault, and Rape: A Theory and Politics of Rape Prevention." *Berkeley Journal of Gender, Law & Justice* 22.1 (2007): 225-130. Web. 25 Mar. 2017.

[63] Cahill, Ann J. "Foucault, Rape, and the Construction of the Feminine Body." *Hypatia* 15.1 (2000): 43-63. *JSTOR [JSTOR].* Web. 1 Mar. 2017.

[64] Cahill, Ann J. "Foucault, Rape, and the Construction of the Feminine Body." *Hypatia* 15.1 (2000): 43-63. *JSTOR [JSTOR].* Web. 1 Mar. 2017.

[65] Cahill, Ann J. "Foucault, Rape, and the Construction of the Feminine Body." *Hypatia* 15.1 (2000): 43-63. *JSTOR [JSTOR].* Web. 1 Mar. 2017.

assault.[66] One may argue that this claim is problematic, for it suggests that rape only occurs when a penis is involved, which is not always necessarily the case. Another problem with this claim derives from Foucault's reference to the penis, which implies that the act of rape is only possible due to male physiology, whereby only women can be raped.[67] But Foucault's point is that rape is in fact about power.[68] Accordingly, when a victim is raped, the rapist exerts power over her. The victim also has the power to fight this act of violence. The issue with Foucault's claim regarding female power during such an instance, however, is that it is only true in theory. Foucault removes and fails to consider any social or cultural context, thus desexualizing rape.[69] He entirely ignores the figurative and literal power disparity between men and women in society. Foucault's understanding of power relations between men and women thus fails to reflect present day realities, despite his intent to put forward legislation to protect women.

2.5 Strategic Rape Concept

Strategic rape concept is currently the leading theory used to explain sexual violence in conflict.[70] According to the strategic rape

---

[66] Cahill, Ann J. "Foucault, Rape, and the Construction of the Feminine Body." *Hypatia* 15.1 (2000): 43-63. *JSTOR [JSTOR]*. Web. 1 Mar. 2017.

[67] Henderson, Holly. "Feminism, Foucault, and Rape: A Theory and Politics of Rape Prevention." *Berkeley Journal of Gender, Law & Justice* 22.1 (2007): 225-130. Web. 25 Mar. 2017.

[68] Henderson, Holly. "Feminism, Foucault, and Rape: A Theory and Politics of Rape Prevention." *Berkeley Journal of Gender, Law & Justice* 22.1 (2007): 225-130. Web. 25 Mar. 2017.

[69] Henderson, Holly. "Feminism, Foucault, and Rape: A Theory and Politics of Rape Prevention." *Berkeley Journal of Gender, Law & Justice* 22.1 (2007): 225-130. Web. 25 Mar. 2017.

[70] Gottschall, Jonathan. "Explaining Wartime Rape." *The Journal of Sex Research* 41.2 (2004): 129-36. *JSTOR*. Web. 21 Apr. 2017.

concept, rape is understood as being "just another ordinance - like bombs, bullets, or propaganda - that a military can use to accomplish its strategic objectives; rape is a tactic executed by soldiers in the service of larger strategic objectives."[71] Sexual violence is thus institutionalized, such that the execution of sexual violence is not random but rather systematic.[72] It is a planned, coordinated, and coherent tactic explicitly laid out by (but not limited to) the highest officers in the chain of command in order to further the military objectives.[73]

Elisabeth Jean Wood has explained what strategic rape entails. Strategic rape is purposefully adopted to attain organizational objectives where it is ordered.[74] Moreover, rape can be used as a strategy of war to cleanse geographic areas of minorities as a form of collective punishment and/or an institutionalized means of reward and compensation for combatants.[75] Wood also states that "when an organization institutionalizes sexual slavery or forced marriage, the organization has purposefully adopted that form of sexual violence in pursuit of organization objectives, and it is therefore a strategy."[76] Wood, however, defines strategic rape differently as she only limits the definition to

---

[71] Gottschall, Jonathan. "Explaining Wartime Rape." *The Journal of Sex Research* 41.2 (2004): 129-36. *JSTOR*. Web. 21 Apr. 2017.
[72] Gottschall, Jonathan. "Explaining Wartime Rape." *The Journal of Sex Research* 41.2 (2004): 129-36. *JSTOR*. Web. 21 Apr. 2017.
[73] Gottschall, Jonathan. "Explaining Wartime Rape." *The Journal of Sex Research* 41.2 (2004): 129-36. *JSTOR*. Web. 21 Apr. 2017.
[74] Wood, Elisabeth Jean. "Conflict-related Sexual Violence and the Policy Implications of Recent Research." *International Review of the Red Cross* 96.894 (2014): 457-78. *JSTOR [JSTOR]*. Web. 2 Apr. 2017.
[75] Wood, Elisabeth Jean. "Conflict-related Sexual Violence and the Policy Implications of Recent Research." *International Review of the Red Cross* 96.894 (2014): 457-78. *JSTOR [JSTOR]*. Web. 2 Apr. 2017.
[76] Wood, Elisabeth Jean. "Conflict-related Sexual Violence and the Policy Implications of Recent Research." *International Review of the Red Cross* 96.894 (2014): 457-78. *JSTOR [JSTOR]*. Web. 2 Apr. 2017.

commanders giving the order to rape.[77] In addition to Wood's definition, unlike what other scholars of strategic rape concept propose, studying variations of rape in conflict is necessary to determine whether it is strategic, opportunistic, or a practice.

Anne Barstow mentioned in her book, *War's Dirty Secret*, that systematic mass rape institutionalized in such conflict areas as in Rwanda and former Yugoslavia in the 1990s was planned, as they were systematic and used to attain certain military and ideological goals.[78] Barstow's book is a comparative analysis of sexual violence in conflicts perpetrated by the Japanese, who institutionalized rape through the use of "comfort women;" Rwandan Hutus, whose forces brutally raped Tutsi women; Kenyans who targeted Kikuyu women; Guatemalans who brutally targeted government opponents with murder and rape; and many other conflicts. Barstow claims that these conflicts proved that women are of strategic importance in warfare. Women have strategic importance, for "whether as 'toilets' (Japanese soldiers' name for comfort women), as surrogates for men's honor, as unwilling child bearers, as (literal) targets, or as prized symbols and measures of how destructive an armed force can be, women now figure regularly in military strategy."[79] This implies that sexual violence against women plays a crucial role in modern conflict. In other words, rape is not just

---

[77] Wood, Elisabeth Jean. "Multiple Perpetrator Rape during War." *Handbook on the Study of Multiple Perpetrator Rape: A Multidisciplinary Response to an International Problem.* Ed. Miranda A. H. Horvath and Jessica Woodhams. London: Routledge, Taylor & Francis, 2013. 132-59. Print.

[78] Barstow, Anne Llewellyn. "Introduction." *War's Dirty Secret: Rape, Prostitution, and Other Crimes against Women.* Ed. Anne Llewellyn. Barstow. Cleveland, OH: Pilgrim, 2000. 1-10. Print.

[79] Barstow, Anne Llewellyn. "Introduction." *War's Dirty Secret: Rape, Prostitution, and Other Crimes against Women.* Ed. Anne Llewellyn. Barstow. Cleveland, OH: Pilgrim, 2000. 1-10. Print.

sexual assault; mass rape has an overreaching effect that extends beyond the chaos of the initial trauma: "as a political weapon, it can change the balance between ethnic, racial, or religious groups."[80] This was the case in Bosnia, where perpetrators attempted to establish ethnic and religious superiority, and where raped women could no longer be mother figures within their respective groups because of inherent cultural shame. This had the effect of altering the regional and local balance of power. Moreover, mass rape policies that include forced impregnation also have many uses, including the destruction of an ethnic group, which was the case in both Bosnia and Rwanda. In both conflicts, forced impregnation was institutionalized to merge ethnic bloodlines and force women to bear children by Christian Serbs and Tutsi men, respectively, - a technique of genocide.[81]

In contrast to the feminist theories, strategic rape concept does not desexualize the act of sexual violence or rape because sexual slavery is partly about the satisfaction of the soldiers' sexual desires so that they can perform better in combat.[82] Moreover, feminist theory states that the rape of unknown women that has no relation to the perpetrator is one of the motives to rape, thus stressing the importance of anonymity. Strategic rape concept holds a different view, that recognition is the main driver, as it was noticed in the Bosnian case that victims would not go back to

---

[80] Barstow, Anne Llewellyn. "Rape as a Weapon of Armed Conflict." *War's Dirty Secret: Rape, Prostitution, and Other Crimes against Women.* Ed. Anne Llewellyn. Barstow. Cleveland, OH: Pilgrim, 2000. 45. Print.

[81] Barstow, Anne Llewellyn. "Rape as a Weapon of Armed Conflict." *War's Dirty Secret: Rape, Prostitution, and Other Crimes against Women.* Ed. Anne Llewellyn. Barstow. Cleveland, OH: Pilgrim, 2000. 45. Print.

[82] Barstow, Anne Llewellyn. "Introduction." *War's Dirty Secret: Rape, Prostitution, and Other Crimes against Women.* Ed. Anne Llewellyn. Barstow. Cleveland, OH: Pilgrim, 2000. 1-10. Print.

their towns or villages if they knew the perpetrators. This unpleasant fact furthered the goal of ethnic cleansing.

2.6 Review of Theories and Concepts

Feminist theory	- Men will rape women given the opportunity. - Men rape women to exercise power. - Men rape in war when the women are unknown (anonymity). - Men sexually enslave women as a measure of power and masculinity - Men rape in war for military reasons such as ethnic cleansing. - Sexual violence has nothing to do with sexuality but rather with power (sexual violence is desexualized). - Rape is based on environmental and social contexts.
Evolution theory	- Men rape for inherited evolutionary reasons. - Men rape out of fear of not being chosen by women, which dims their chances of reproductive success. - Men rape due to a biological urge to procreate. - Evolution theory ignores or minimizes social context.
Strategic rape concept	- Rape is strategic in that it aids in reaching end goals, such as eliminating a targeted group or forcibly displacing them from a targeted area. - Men rape in conflict due to sexual desire, which helps them perform better (sexualizing the act of rape). - Strategic rape is planned and institutionalized to reach a military objective. - Familiarity can be a motive to rape in war because victims may not return to their town or village because they might know their attacker.

2.7 Gaps in Knowledge

The first gap is that there is no consensus on why men rape in war because the motives for sexual violence in conflict is never monocausal. One theory cannot apply to all cases, nor can it predict behaviors due to variations in sexual violence in conflict. The necessity of addressing this gap is to justify that the most influential theories pertaining to the explanation of why sexual violence occur do not exclusively apply, indicating that further research should be carried out in order to test other concepts' explanatory strengths and to deploy better policies to address the issue (no root cause= no solution).

The second gap arises from the case study, which reveals a lack of theological discourse addressing sexual violence and institutionalized by ideology or religion. This gap is relevant to analyzing ISIS's use of sexual violence in light of the group's justification of the act of enslaving Yezidi women, which was elaborated by its department of research, and in jurisprudence that rested on the group's interpretation of sharia law and other religious sources, such as hadith and the Koran.

The third gap is the lack of primary sources on sexual violence due to the sensitivity of topic. However, the more primary data becomes available, the more accurate the research will become.

2.8 Other Concepts and Explanations

Although the leading explanations for sexual violence in conflict have been reviewed, it is important to consider a few more concepts that are worth looking into. These include variations of sexual violence and religious-ideological elements.

2.8.1 Variations of Sexual Violence During War

Sexual violence occurs in most wars, but it comes in different forms and occurs with varying degrees of effect. In other words, in some conflicts sexual violence is widespread, and in other conflicts sexual violence is limited. Sometimes sexual violence that is widespread is committed at random and holds no strategic importance, while in some conflicts sexual violence is a means to an end.[83] There is a widespread misconception that sexual violence is limited to ethnic conflicts. This has the detrimental effect of over-predicting sexual violence in conflict based on insufficient evidence. It also fails in practice. The civil war in Sri Lanka and Israeli-Palestinian conflict, for example, were/are ethnic in nature but had/have only rare incidents of sexual violence.[84] While sexual violence is not synonymous with ethnic conflict, highlighting the misconception to the contrary emphasizes the importance of context, which should draw individual analysis. Elisabeth Jean Wood argues that "sexual violence varies in prevalence and form across civil wars as well as inter-state wars, across ethnic wars as well as non-ethnic, and across secessionist conflicts."[85] Wood further explains that the concept of "repertoire" is essential for analyzing variation of wartime rape. She defines repertoire of violence as "the subset of battle death, assassination, forced displacement, torture, the various forms of sexual violence, and so

---

[83] Wood, Elisabeth Jean. "Variation in Sexual Violence during War." *Politics & Society* 34.3 (2006): 307-41. *Politics & Society*. Sage Publications, Sept. 2006. Web. 25 Mar. 2017.
[84] Wood, Elisabeth Jean. "Variation in Sexual Violence during War." *Politics & Society* 34.3 (2006): 307-41. *Politics & Society*. Sage Publications, Sept. 2006. Web. 25 Mar. 2017.
[85] Wood, Elisabeth Jean. "Variation in Sexual Violence during War." *Politics & Society* 34.3 (2006): 307-41. *Politics & Society*. Sage Publications, Sept. 2006. Web. 25 Mar. 2017.

on regularly observed on the part of the armed group."[86] This implies that the concept focuses on the differences in perpetrated acts. [87] Moreover, repertoires are not uniform. They can be wide or narrow, effective or ineffective; in other words, some armed groups engage in mass rape while others do not.[88]

Repertoire entails frequency, target, and purpose. These three elements of repertoire are used to measure the variation of sexual violence. Frequency of sexual violence refers to how often it occurs. In qualitative terms, it is important to label this frequency as "very frequent," "moderately often," or "rarely."[89] Frequency is generally measured by comparing the frequency of sexual violence or rape committed by one group compared to another group.[90] Frequency is measured via various methods, depending on the focus of measurement. For example, "the number of events (rapes for example), the number of events per member of the referent population (incidence),

---

[86] Wood, Elisabeth Jean. "Multiple Perpetrator Rape during War." *Handbook on the Study of Multiple Perpetrator Rape: A Multidisciplinary Response to an International Problem*. Ed. Miranda A. H. Horvath and Jessica Woodhams. London: Routledge, Taylor & Francis, 2013. 132-59. Print.

[87] Wood, Elisabeth Jean. "Multiple Perpetrator Rape during War." *Handbook on the Study of Multiple Perpetrator Rape: A Multidisciplinary Response to an International Problem*. Ed. Miranda A. H. Horvath and Jessica Woodhams. London: Routledge, Taylor & Francis, 2013. 132-59. Print.

[88] Wood, Elisabeth Jean. "Multiple Perpetrator Rape during War." *Handbook on the Study of Multiple Perpetrator Rape: A Multidisciplinary Response to an International Problem*. Ed. Miranda A. H. Horvath and Jessica Woodhams. London: Routledge, Taylor & Francis, 2013. 132-59. Print.

[89] Wood, Elisabeth Jean. "Multiple Perpetrator Rape during War." *Handbook on the Study of Multiple Perpetrator Rape: A Multidisciplinary Response to an International Problem*. Ed. Miranda A. H. Horvath and Jessica Woodhams. London: Routledge, Taylor & Francis, 2013. 132-59. Print.

[90] Wood, Elisabeth Jean. "Multiple Perpetrator Rape during War." *Handbook on the Study of Multiple Perpetrator Rape: A Multidisciplinary Response to an International Problem*. Ed. Miranda A. H. Horvath and Jessica Woodhams. London: Routledge, Taylor & Francis, 2013. 132-59. Print.

or the fraction of the referent population that suffered at least once such event (prevalence)"[91] are all possible means of measuring frequency.

2.8.2 The Religious-Ideological Element

This element should be investigated because ISIS explicitly referred to religious ideology to justify its victimization of the Yezidis' suffering from sexual violence. It would be ambitious to look into this gap as it requires a study by itself, however this element will be briefly discussed in Chapter 6.

---

[91] Wood, Elisabeth Jean. "Multiple Perpetrator Rape during War." *Handbook on the Study of Multiple Perpetrator Rape: A Multidisciplinary Response to an International Problem*. Ed. Miranda A. H. Horvath and Jessica Woodhams. London: Routledge, Taylor & Francis, 2013. 132-59. Print.

Chapter 3:
Background Information

This chapter will provide background on both ISIS and the Yezidi community. It is important to note that there will only be a brief history of ISIS, as this research aims to understand ISIS's use of sexual violence, and an extensive history of ISIS would be too lengthy and include many elements that fall beyond the scope of this book.

3.1 ISIS

ISIS is an acronym for the so-called Islamic State of Syria and Iraq. It is also known by its Arabic name, Da'esh, and by the more formal designation, "Islamic State in Iraq and the Levant" (ISIL).[92] Until very recently, it claimed the "leadership of the global jihadist movement," overshadowing Al Qaeda Central (AQC), which was responsible for the September 11, 2001 attacks on the United States, among other terrorist acts on American assets worldwide. However, ISIS did not just parachute into Iraq and Syria, as Fawaz Gerges puts it in his book *ISIS: A History*.[93] ISIS arose from the same "Salafist-Jihadist"

---

[92] Gerges, Fawaz A. "Down the Rabbit Hole and into the History of ISIS." Introduction. *ISIS: A History*. Princeton, NJ: Princeton UP, 2017. 1-22. Print.
[93] Gerges, Fawaz A. *ISIS: A History*. Princeton, NJ: Princeton UP, 2017. Print.

family that has given birth"[94] to the likes of the "Egyptian Islamic jihad, Al Qaeda Central (AQC), Al Qaeda in Iraq (AQI), and Al Qaeda in the Arabian Peninsula (AQAP) over the past three decades."[95] In other words, "it is the extension of the global salafist-jihadist movement."[96] By May 2010 a group within AQI had come under the leadership of the Iraqi religious scholar Abu Bakr al-Baghdadi under the name the Islamic State of Iraq (ISI). Three years later it became ISIL and, then, on June 29, 2014, proclaimed itself a Caliphate under al-Baghdadi's supreme leadership. Under any name, ISIS has not been completely unique in its behavior; in fact it has many similarities with its predecessors and current competitors, including its display of public executions, a spectacle of violence pioneered by AQI.[97] The major difference is ISIS's heightened use of extreme violence displayed for the public as a means of deterrence to its enemies and as a means of a recruitment strategy showcasing strength and dominance.[98] Another obvious difference is that none of the previous or current Salafist-jihadi groups controlled territories in the manner of a government, as ISIS managed to do for several years over broad swaths of Iraq and Syria.[99]

---

[94] Gerges, Fawaz A. "Acknowledgements." Preface. *ISIS: A History*. Princeton, NJ: Princeton UP, 2017. Xv-Xix. Print.
[95] Gerges, Fawaz A. "Acknowledgements." Preface. *ISIS: A History*. Princeton, NJ: Princeton UP, 2017. Xv-Xix. Print.
[96] Gerges, Fawaz A. "The World According to ISIS." *ISIS: A History*. Princeton, NJ: Princeton UP, 2017. 23-49. Print.
[97] Gerges, Fawaz A. "Acknowledgements." Preface. *ISIS: A History*. Princeton, NJ: Princeton UP, 2017. Xv-Xix. Print.
[98] Gerges, Fawaz A. "Acknowledgements." Preface. *ISIS: A History*. Princeton, NJ: Princeton UP, 2017. Xv-Xix. Print.
[99] Hashim, Ahmed S. "Understanding the Islamic State." *The Caliphate at War: The Ideological, Organisational and Military Innovations of Islamic State*. London: Hurst, 2016. 3-16. Print.

Roughly from 2013 to 2017, ISIS controlled an area of Iraq and Syria almost as large as the United Kingdom, including a population of more than six million people.[100] ISIS's Blitzkrieg proved a rude awakening to the regional powers as an army of few thousand fighters took Mosul, Iraq's second largest city of two million inhabitants, and Syria's Raqqa, a city that strategically sits on the Euphrates.[101]

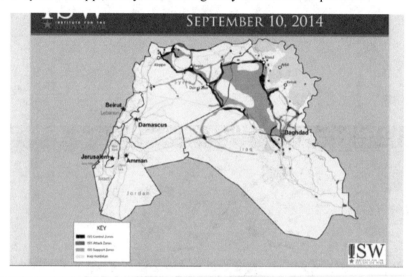

---

[100] Gerges, Fawaz A. "Down the Rabbit Hole and into the History of ISIS." Introduction. *ISIS: A History*. Princeton, NJ: Princeton UP, 2017. 1-22. Print.
[101] Gerges, Fawaz A. "Down the Rabbit Hole and into the History of ISIS." Introduction. *ISIS: A History*. Princeton, NJ: Princeton UP, 2017. 1-22. Print.

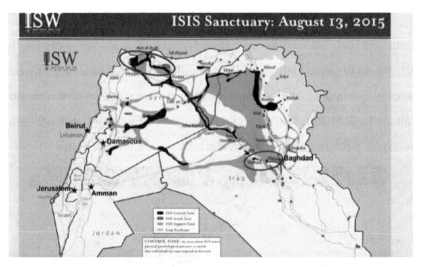

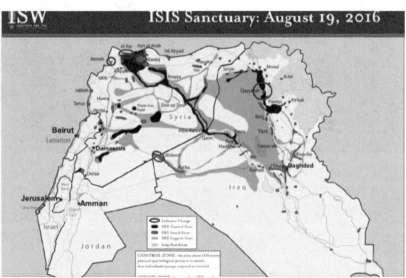

ISIS proved that it was able to defeat the Iraqi, Kurdish, and Syrian armed forces in significant battles. This alarmed Western powers, who feared that neighboring Jordan, Lebanon, and Saudi Arabia were the likely next targets.[102] ISIS victories caused numerous Islamist groups

---

[102] Gerges, Fawaz A. "Down the Rabbit Hole and into the History of ISIS." Introduction. *ISIS: A History*. Princeton, NJ: Princeton UP, 2017. 1-22. Print.

around the globe to swear allegiance. These included Boko Haram in Nigeria, Islamist militias in Libya, the Ansar Beit al-Maqdis group in Sinai in Egypt, jihadist groups in Yemen, Taliban defectors in Afghanistan, groups in Saudi Arabia, and groups in the North Caucasus region of Russia.[103] The groups that have sworn allegiance created their own *villayat*, or emirates, which have claimed to adhere to ISIS's long-term agenda.

ISIS's ideology, which focuses on a hyper-Sunni identity, adds fuel to the existing Sunni-Shia rift in the Middle East and beyond.[104] Regardless of its organizational identity, its main campaign slogan is "fundamentally oriented toward a genocidal anti-Shia campaign conducted in the name of the romantic idea of resurrecting the caliphate."[105] ISIS's brutality is directed toward any entity that sees the world differently in a way that strips the "other" of human dignity. Shia Muslims, Christian, and Jews are already considered infidels but are seen as "people of the book" who may be permitted to live under strictures of Islamist rule that date back to the Middle Ages, notably including payment of a special tax (*jizya*) required of non-Muslims. For other religious minorities, including the Yezidis, these arrangements are insufficient. According to ISIS's ideology, the Yezidis are pagan "devil worshippers." In both theory and practice, their men should be slaughtered and their women enslaved. ISIS's institutionalized violence

---

[103] Boghani, Priyanka. "Where the Black Flag of ISIS Flies A Look at the Nine Countries Where the Terror Group Has Formal Affiliates." *Where the Black Flag of ISIS Flies*. PBS, 13 May 2016. Web. 25 May 2018.
[104] Gerges, Fawaz A. "The World According to ISIS." *ISIS: A History.* Princeton, NJ: Princeton UP, 2017. 23-49. Print.
[105] Gerges, Fawaz A. "The World According to ISIS." *ISIS: A History.* Princeton, NJ: Princeton UP, 2017. 23-49. Print.

is even justified and communicated to all of ISIS's followers through their propaganda magazine *Dabiq* and Islamic jurisprudence experts from the *shura* council.[106]

An article in the second issue of *Dabiq* titled "The Revival of Slavery Before the Hour" stipulates that ISIS's conquests faced it with a population of pagans - the Yezidis. The articles maintain that "their continuous existence to this day is a matter that Muslims should question as they will be asked about it on Judgment Day, considering that Allah had revealed the *Ayat as-sayf* [verse of the sword] over 1400 years ago." This verse, which is taken out of context, stipulates that "when the sacred months have passed, then kill the *mushrikin* [idolators] wherever you find them, and capture them, and besiege them, and sit in wait for them at every place of ambush. But if they should repent, establish prayer, and give *zakah* [alms], let them go their way." However, the article proceeded to explain that after carefully assessing whether the Yezidis are idolators (*mushrikin*) or apostates (*fuqaha*), its experts ruled that the Yezidis would not enjoy the same option as Christians and Jews to pay a tax (*jizya*) for toleration. The article further explains that since they are considered devil worshippers, their women "could be enslaved and can only be given an ultimatum to repent or face the sword."[107]

The blatant indoctrination and institutionalization of violence against the Yezidi people went beyond the mere words that ISIS used to incite and justify the violence itself. "The trade in Yezidi women and girls has created a persistent infrastructure, with a network of warehouses where the victims are held, viewing rooms where they are inspected and

---

[106] Gerges, Fawaz A. "The World According to ISIS." *ISIS: A History*. Princeton, NJ: Princeton UP, 2017. 23-49. Print.
[107] *Dabiq*

marketed, and a dedicated fleet of buses used to transport them."[108] ISIS set up an administrative department of "War Spoils" to manage its modern sex slave trade, which consisted of sales contracts notarized by ISIS-run Islamic courts.[109] There was even a price list of children aged one to nine, starting at around $165 and decreasing with age. In some cases, victims were sold back to their families for thousands of dollars in ransom, thus proving that this practice also falls in line with ISIS's revenue-driven economic model. Moreover, the sex trade was also an effective recruiting tool attracting men from highly conservative Muslim communities, where casual sexual relations are taboo.[110] The promise of women was also exploited to lure men into the Caliphate. A call for "sexual jihad" led an estimated 500 Western women to travel to ISIS territories in Syria and Iraq.

The aforementioned institutionalization of sexual slavery was not solely based on the gender power politics and the dominance of patriarchy. According to Fawaz, the use of violence against the Yezidis was also driven by "ideological zealousness"[111] because al Baghdadi and his *shura* council "want[ed] to distinguish themselves from Islamist rivals by attempting to revive traditions, rituals, and practices that have

---

[108] Callimachi, Rukmini. "ISIS Enshrines a Theology of Rape." *The New York Times*. The New York Times, 13 Aug. 2015. Web. 4 Aug. 2018. <https://www.nytimes.com/2015/08/14/world/middleeast/isis-enshrines-a-theology-of-rape.html>.

[109] Gerges, Fawaz A. "The World According to ISIS." *ISIS: A History*. Princeton, NJ: Princeton UP, 2017. 23-49. Print.

[110] Gerges, Fawaz A. "The World According to ISIS." *ISIS: A History*. Princeton, NJ: Princeton UP, 2017. 23-49. Print.

[111] Gerges, Fawaz A. "The World According to ISIS." *ISIS: A History*. Princeton, NJ: Princeton UP, 2017. 23-49. Print.

been dormant for a thousand years in Muslim history."[112] This purported emulation of the Prophet is important for the image of religious purity and authenticity they are eager to promote.

3.2 The Yezidi Women

"Y[e]zidism," according to one definition, "is an ancient monotheistic religion, spread orally by holy men entrusted with our stories. It has elements in common with the many religions of the Middle East, from Mithraism and Zoroastrianism to Islam and Judaism."[113] In addition to surviving as one of Iraq's oldest religious minorities, there are said to be around 700,000 Yezidis worldwide, with only the highest concentration living in northern Iraq.[114] Although the religion's founder is unknown, the key belief of the Yezidis is that "the integrity of the religion was preserved through the trans-migration of souls,"[115] in other words reincarnation. Yezidis are monotheistic and believe in one God, whom they call "Khuda." According to the Yezidi tradition, "the task of creation and the establishment of plant and animal life on earth was assigned to seven angels, of whom the greatest was Azaziel."[116] Although the story of Azaziel's refusal to bow down before Adam

---

[112] Gerges, Fawaz A. "The World According to ISIS." *ISIS: A History.* Princeton, NJ: Princeton UP, 2017. 23-49. Print.

[113] Murad, Nadia. "Chapter 1." *The Last Girl: My Story of Captivity, and My Fight against the Islamic State.* 1st ed. New York: Tim Duggan, 2017. 3-14. Print.

[114] Jalabi, Raya. "Who Are the Yazidis and Why Is Isis Hunting Them?" The Guardian. Guardian News and Media, 11 Aug. 2014. Web. 25 May 2018.

[115] Guest, John S. "The Yezidi Religion." The Yezidis: A Study in Survival. London: Routledge & Kegan Paul, Associated Book (UK)Ltd., 1987. 28-41. Print.

[116] Guest, John S. "The Yezidi Religion." The Yezidis: A Study in Survival. London: Routledge & Kegan Paul, Associated Book (UK)Ltd., 1987. 28-41. Print.

follows parallel narratives in the Jewish, Christian, and Muslim traditions, in which Azaziel was banished and is widely identified as the fallen angel that is synonymous with evil, the Yezidis have a different narrative.[117] They believe that God forgave Azaziel's act of disobedience and that recognizing the angel as supreme will grant them special protection. Yezidis do not normally use the name Azaziel, but instead use the title of Melek Taus (Peacock Angel), hence the representation of a peacock as the Yezedi emblem.[118]

The Yezidi community is conservative. Casual romantic relations outside the bounds of marriage are frowned upon, and the sanctity of unwed girls is extremely important for the honor of individual girls, their families, and the community. Yezidis are strictly endogamous and not allowed to marry outside their faith, nor can anyone convert to Yezidism.

The Yezidis' misunderstood religion has led many of their neighbors to believe that they are devil worshippers and therefore deserve to die. They were able to withstand seventy-two attempted genocides under Ottoman rule alone,[119] surviving thanks to their isolated

---

[117] Guest, John S. "The Yezidi Religion." *The Yezidis: A Study in Survival.* London: Routledge & Kegan Paul, Associated Book (UK)Ltd., 1987. 28-41. Print.

[118] Guest, John S. "The Yezidi Religion." *The Yezidis: A Study in Survival.* London: Routledge & Kegan Paul, Associated Book (UK)Ltd., 1987. 28-41. Print.

[119] Jalabi, Raya. "Who Are the Yazidis and Why Is Isis Hunting Them?" *The Guardian.* Guardian News and Media, 11 Aug. 2014. Web. 25 May 2018.

location in Mount Sinjar region.[120] As recently as 2007, AQI killed approximately 800 Yezidis after denouncing them as infidels.[121]

---

[120] Fuccaro, Nelida. *Aspects of the Social and Political History of the Yazidi Enclave of Jabal Sinjar (Iraq) under the British Mandate, 1919-1932*. Thesis. Durham University, 1994. Durham: Durham Theses, 1994. Print.

[121] Jalabi, Raya. "Who Are the Yazidis and Why Is Isis Hunting Them?" *The Guardian*. Guardian News and Media, 11 Aug. 2014. Web. 25 May 2018.

Chapter 4:
Methodology

4.1 Main Research Question

This book's main research question is: How can ISIS's use of sexual violence against Yezidi women in Iraq since August 2014 be explained? Sexual violence in conflict, and in this study's context, follows the United Nations definition, that is, any act of "rape, sexual slavery, forced prostitution, forced pregnancy, forced abortion, enforced sterilization, forced marriage, [sexual trafficking] and any other form of sexual violence of comparable gravity perpetrated against women, men, girls or boys that is directly or indirectly linked to a conflict."[122]

4.2 Research Methods

The research method chosen for this research is qualitative. Qualitative research mainly focuses on the goal of delivering meaning to a phenomenon and its complexities. In contrast, quantitative research uses deductive reasoning to derive at a definitive answer through the use of positivist social science methods such as surveys, statistics, etc., which can lead to generalizations that often overlook the importance of context.

---

[122] Office of the Special Representative of the Secretary-General on Sexual Violence in Conflict. *Report of the Secretary-General on Conflict-Related Sexual Violence*. Rep. no. 249. United Nations, 15 Apr. 2017. Web.

Qualitative research also focuses on observations of behavior, processes, and events, which compliments the nature of the main research question. Additionally, qualitative research allows for greater flexibility, which is of great use for addressing a relatively new and on-going issue.

4.3 Research Design

"The research design links the data to be collected (and to the conclusions to be drawn) to the initial questions of study."[123] In other words, it links the abstract to the concrete. The unit of analysis chosen in this research is ISIS's use of sexual violence and the unit of observation is the Yezidi women in Iraq who survived and escaped ISIS sexual slavery since August 2014. The type of study employed in this research is a single case study research. I chose the single case study type for numerous reasons. First, it the main research question focuses entirely on sexual violence ISIS inflicted on Yezidi women in Iraq. It is important to specify these parameters because Iraq was in an on-going conflict for many years that also extended to Syria. Sexual violence against women and men during the conflicts in both countries have been extensively reported. It was therefore of greater utility to limit the study to one country, one period, one unit of observation, and one unit of analysis.

4.3.1 Legitimation of Research Design: Single Case Study

Case Study "research is an in-depth examination of an excessive amount of information about very few units or cases for one period or

---

[123] Yin, Robert K. "Designing Case Studies Identifying Your Case(s) and Establishing the Logic of Your Case Study." *Case Study Research and Applications: Design and Methods.* 6th ed. Los Angeles, CA: SAGE, 2018. 24-80. Print.

across multiple periods of time."[124] Moreover, this type of research thoroughly investigates one or more small sets of cases by concentrating on each case's intricate features and context,[125] thus creating a nexus between the individual actions to the bigger picture (micro to macro).

According to such research experts as W. Lawrence Neuman, case study research is the most preferable for a new topic, which makes this investigation's subject an ideal candidate for the use of case-study research.[126] According to Neuman's book *Social Research Methods: Qualitative and Quantitative Approaches*,[127] case studies are also highly preferable since they usually lead to in-depth understanding of the topic and offer numerous advantages, including conceptual validity, heuristic effect, causal mechanisms identification, and the ability to capture complexity and trace processes, calibration, and holistic elaboration. Robert K. Yin notes that the need for a case study "arises out of the desire to understand complex and social phenomena"[128] as they provide holistic views via in-depth analysis.

---

[124] Neuman, W. Lawrence. "What Are the Major Types of Social Research?" *Social Research Methods: Qualitative and Quantitative Approaches: Pearson New International Edition*. Harlow: Pearson Education Limited, 2014. 25-54. Print.

[125] Neuman, W. Lawrence. "What Are the Major Types of Social Research?" *Social Research Methods: Qualitative and Quantitative Approaches: Pearson New International Edition*. Harlow: Pearson Education Limited, 2014. 25-54. Print.

[126] Neuman, W. Lawrence. "What Are the Major Types of Social Research?" *Social Research Methods:Qualitative and Quantitative Approaches: Pearson New International Edition*. Harlow: Pearson Education Limited, 2014. 25-54. Print.

[127] Neuman, W. Lawrence. *Social Research Methods: Qualitative and Quantitative Appraoches*. 7th ed. Essex: Pearson Education Limited, 2014. Print.

[128] Yin, Robert K. *Case Study Research and Applications: Design and Methods*. 6th ed. Thousand Oaks, CA: SAGE Publications, 2018. Print.

It is important to note that it is impossible to generalize human actions or practices. The objective of the study is to test the theories that are applied. This study's aim is not to generalize the population of cases, but to generalize the theory. Having one conclusion fitting one case is not frowned upon in the study and the understanding of sexual violence in conflict, as each situation is somewhat unique.

Although case study research boasts numerous strengths, it also suffers from certain vulnerabilities.[129] Yin suggests that multiple-case studies tend to produce outcomes that avoid replication and bear more credibility than single-case studies. Nevertheless, single case studies offer invaluable insights. It is also difficult to maintain that a single-case study is vulnerable without referring to the context. Multiple-case studies could even have been counterproductive for this particular project, for the gap in knowledge results in significant part from scholarly attempts to identify one primary explanation of why sexual violence occurs. This tends to disregard context and fails to acknowledge that each act of sexual violence varies with respect to repertoire and motive. It is also worth mentioning that the Yezidis are unique because there are no other cases in which ISIS inflicted, as a systematic matter of policy, sexual violence against another ethnic minority in Iraq, or anywhere else, particularly with enough data or access to data. Moreover, as mentioned earlier, the objective of this single-case study is to test the theories that were laid in chapter two. Therefore, the single-case study is the most

---

[129] Yin, Robert K. "Designing Case Studies Identifying Your Case(s) and Establishing the Logic of Your Case Study." *Case Study Research and Applications: Design and Methods.* 6th ed. Los Angeles, CA: SAGE, 2018. 24-80. Print.

suitable type of research applicable to study how ISIS used sexual violence.

4.4 Data Collection Methods

This section will provide a clear outline of the type of data necessary to answer the main research question. It will also discuss the methods used to obtain data. The first sub-section will cover secondary data, the methods utilized to obtain it, and its relevance to the study. The second sub-section will address the use of primary data and the methods used to obtain it. The third sub-section will discuss how that the data was analyzed. By way of general introduction, data collection methods included open-ended interviews, elite interviews, fieldwork, and empirical research.

4.4.1 Secondary Data and Collection Method

Secondary data began with empirical research to obtain a preliminary understanding of the topic. It also helped assess how much work has been done in order to determine what new data is needed to fill any lacunae in extant knowledge. Moreover, secondary sources are integral and inseparable components of this study since they provide guidance with regard to what information is available and support a better understanding of the primary sources.

Secondary sources include academic books and articles and media articles. Documentary collections and archival records have some weaknesses, such as the difficulty in retrieving the necessary documents

from a troubled region, biased selectivity, and privacy protections.[130]
Some of these problems were addressed by finding numerous sources
that have different narratives or views on the topic with regards to the
theories and concepts used to explain sexual violence in conflict. As for
information derived from media sources, the narrative was more or else
similar through the majority of outlets with regard to the chain of events.
It is also important to keep in mind that even though documentation can
be useful and reliable, it is not necessarily accurate.[131] According Yin,
"documents must be carefully used and not to be accepted as literal
recordings of events that have taken place."[132]

4.4.2 Primary Data and Collection Method

Primary sources offer invaluable insights, particularly when a
topic is understudied and current. Primary data is by definition collected
first hand for a specific research purpose.[133] A primary source can be
"published (e.g. census data) or unpublished (e.g. President Lincoln's
personal diary), and could be from the past (e.g. artifacts) or present (e.g.

---

[130] in, Robert K. "Collecting Case Study Evidence- The Principles You Should
Follow in Working With Six Sources of Evidence." *Case Study Research and
Applications: Design and Methods.* 6th ed. Los Angeles: SAGE, 2018. 110-63.
Print.
[131] in, Robert K. "Collecting Case Study Evidence- The Principles You Should
Follow in Working With Six Sources of Evidence." *Case Study Research and
Applications: Design and Methods.* 6th ed. Los Angeles: SAGE, 2018. 110-63.
Print.
[132] in, Robert K. "Collecting Case Study Evidence- The Principles You Should
Follow in Working With Six Sources of Evidence." *Case Study Research and
Applications: Design and Methods.* 6th ed. Los Angeles: SAGE, 2018. 110-63.
Print.
[133] Persaud, Nadini. "Primary Data Source." *Encyclopedia of Research Design.*
Ed. Neil J. Salkind. Thousand Oaks: SAGE Publications, 2012. 1095-097. Print.

poll for a national election)."[134] Moreover, a primary source can also entail recollections of events described by eyewitnesses, or by individuals who experienced the said event. Primary sources and primary data thus provide information that is as close as possible to the subject and to being unmediated.[135] However, primary data do have shortcomings that cannot be ignored. Sometimes the primary data can be inaccurate, due to such factors as dishonesty, inaccurate memories, or bias. This is one of the reasons why fact checking is an important second step when collecting the data. In this research, fieldwork, open-ended interviews, and semi-structured interviews were used to collect primary data. The interviews were primarily with Kurdish government officials, victims, activists, and experts in northern Iraq and beyond.

4.4.2.1 Fieldwork

Field work is "qualitative research in which the researcher directly observes and records notes on people in a natural setting for an extended period of time."[136] Although typical field research might last for a few months or years, it was impossible for me to spend more than three weeks in Iraq due to the security situation, which will be further discussed in the limitations of the study. Field work is usually used in order to obtain in-depth information regarding a group in a certain setting

---

[134] Persaud, Nadini. "Primary Data Source." *Encyclopedia of Research Design.* Ed. Neil J. Salkind. Thousand Oaks: SAGE Publications, 2012. 1095-097. Print.
[135] Persaud, Nadini. "Primary Data Source." *Encyclopedia of Research Design.* Ed. Neil J. Salkind. Thousand Oaks: SAGE Publications, 2012. 1095-097. Print.
[136] Neuman, W. Lawrence. "What Are the Major Types of Social Research?" *Social Research Methods:Qualitative and Quantitative Approaches: Pearson New International Edition.* Harlow: Pearson Education Limited, 2014. 25-54. Print.

or location.[137] This method of research helps in answering "how" and "what" questions (for example, how can we explain x behavior in this country?). Although field research is normally used for descriptive or exploratory research, it is also in some cases used for explanatory cases, which is the case in this research.

4.4.2.2 Open-Ended and Semi-Structured Interviews

The majority of the primary data informing this study comes from the use of semi-structured and open-ended interviews. Interviews offer insights and access to extensive information, especially those with a flexible structure, which was integral for this research. This method also offers a glimpse into how the perception of the topic is created by the subjects themselves. The technique that was used was conversational interviewing, a suitable method because of the sensitivity of the topic and related questions. When interview conversations turned informal, the interviewees opened up and shared more details as there was greater interpersonal trust. This included information that could not have been found easily or at all on the internet or in other sources. As previously mentioned, interviews present some weaknesses, such as bias due to poorly articulated questions, response bias, inaccuracies due to poor recall, and reflexivity.[138] These issues were dealt with in various ways, such as the use of recording to ensure accurate reportage, the articulation

---

[137] Neuman, W. Lawrence. "Field Research and Focus Group Research." *Social Research Methods: Qualitative and Quantitative Approaches: Pearson New International Edition*. Harlow: Pearson Education Limited, 2014. 431-76. Print.
[138] Yin, Robert K. "Collecting Case Study Evidence- The Principles You Should Follow in Working With Six Sources of Evidence." *Case Study Research and Applications: Design and Methods*. 6th ed. Los Angeles: SAGE, 2018. 110-63. Print.

of questions in Arabic, and the use of a conversational format. Biases in a setting like an Internally Displaced Persons (IDP) camp for Yezidis in Iraq are inescapable, and the answers will most probably – and understandably -- be biased in some way. With regard to reflexivity, I informed all of my subjects that I am only a student and that their identities will only be privy to myself and my supervisor. This made the subjects much more comfortable and they spoke freely.

4.4.2.3 Participant Recruitment Method

The first type of interviews included subjects who were directly connected to the Yezidi genocide, mainly including survivors of sexual violence committed by ISIS, Yezidis who lost family members, Yezidi activists, and members of the Kurdish armed forces operating in the region. The second type of interviews included experts, including Yezidi scholar Khidr Domle, sexual violence expert Elizabeth Jean Wood, and a former ICTY prosecutor. A total of 16 interviews was conducted for this project.

Strategies had to be employed to secure those interviews. Prior to my field work, I had to create my own network via a strategy called "snowball sampling." Snowball sampling, or chain referral, is a non-probability sampling method in which you begin with one or two contacts and, via referral from those contacts, build a larger network.[139] This technique is useful for gaining access to populations such as the Yezidi women survivors, who were rather difficult to gain access to.

---

[139] Neuman, W. Lawrence. "Qualitative and Quantitative Sampling." *Social Research Methods: Qualitative and Quantitative Approaches: Pearson New International Edition*. Harlow: Pearson Education Limited, 2014. 246-80. Print.

I arrived in northern Iraq on the August 8, 2016. Prior to embarking on my field trip, I have already set up a network of people who helped me with my stay and research in Iraq. The network of people began with Saadoon Shafi, a politician and senior member of the Patriotic Union of Kurdistan (PUK) who previously served as advisor to president Jalal Talabani). My other point of reference was Wietse Van den Berge, a researcher at the Institute of Security and Global Affairs at Leiden University. Van den Berge put me in contact with Alla Rafiq, a professor at Salahddine University in Irbil, Iraq. Professor Rafiq referred me to two other contacts, Kermanj Othman, Senior Legal Advisor to the Independent Human Rights Commission, and Hussam Salim, Director of Yezidi Organization for Documentation. Helen Hughes, a United Nations official who became a contact via personal relations, referred me to Nabeela Sweisat, a coordinator at the United Nations Higher Commission for Refugees (UNHCR), and Veronica Njikho who is also a coordinator at the United National Population Fun (UNFPA). Raya Barazanji, another personal contact, referred me to Rebwar Bilbas of the Women Empowerment Organization (WEO) and to Liza Hido, president of the Baghdad Women Association (BWA). Hido helped me bypass bureaucratic red tape and placed me in contact with Khidr Domle, a well-known Yezidi public intellectual and researcher. Shayan Talabani, still another personal contact, referred me to Nawaf Ashur, who placed me in contact with Melisande Genat, a Ph.D. candidate at Stanford University who was also a volunteer at Yazda in Dohuk.

After two months of building my network, I left for Iraq. When I arrived, I did not receive any clearance to access the camps, and given my experience in the Middle East, it is pointless to try and get your access prior to arrival, as procedures tend to be lax and slow. Therefore, I attempted to arrange my access in person. During my first two hours in Iraq, a family friend referred me to Major General Ahmed of the Kurdish Peshmerga forces. General Ahmed then referred me to the camp director of the Kurdish region, who asked not to be mentioned. Within a few hours I received my clearance and went to the first IDP camp an hour and a half outside of Irbil. Although the Debaga camp housed no Yezidi women, it was a temporary home for displaced people who had lived under ISIS rule for more than two years. The people I met were mostly from Mosul, Ramadi, or Baaji. It was important to observe and interview them because it gave insight on what the situation was like and reaffirmed my concern with respect to reports coming from agencies such as the UN as they did not have a substantial presence in the camp. That led me to be skeptical of the data in the reports, for the numbers and statistics are difficult to measure in Iraq for many reasons, including the inaccurate numbers with respect to the population (Iraq's last census was in the 1970s). I had some interview questions prepared but as I began questioning my interviewees, they felt ill at ease and were unable to answer questions directly. I thus changed my style on the spot and opted for conversational interviewing, which proved more fruitful. In addition to acquiring insight, it was also important to evaluate not only what ISIS did to the Yezidi population but also to the Sunni population that was living under ISIS rule.

4.4.3 Data Presentation and Analysis

The acquired data will be presented in a narrative format. The narrative will reflect the stories of how the Yezidi women were enslaved and their perception of why they were enslaved. Other interviewees were directly involved or affected by ISIS and its actions and policies. The choice to present the findings in a narrative form is based on the importance of showcasing the raw reality of the situation. There was also no other way to present my findings with authenticity and to respect interviewees by making sure their story is being heard in full.

4.4.3.1 Data Analysis

I used a deductive approach since my main goal was to test competing theories and identify new elements and factors explaining sexual violence. I began by seeking the presence of indicators reflecting the different theories. I then examined the indicators related to new factors such as religion and geopolitics. Lastly, I looked at new elements and factors that could come up during the research and have explanatory strength. In other words, the data was analyzed via coding the empirical information in pre-established indicators, derived from theories and new elements, while also coding any new factors. This method of analysis helped my form a valid statement about the explanatory quality of the main theories, new factors, and some unexpected results.

The tables on the next pages provide the operationalization of the theories, which was the basis of coding the empirical data. The table's functionality will be seen in Chapters Five and Six, in which the findings will be presented and analyzed, respectively.

Theory	Concept	Conceptual Definition	Indicators	Assessment
Evolution Theory	Sexual desire	Sexual desire is a common motivation for human rape and this desire ultimately traces back to men's evolved sexual psychology.	Any phrase or statement by the interviewee or text in document referring to urge or if it was implies that men have sexual needs, especially in war.	Looking into indicators in relevant text and interviews.
	Proximate causation	The immediate causes that operate over a short period of time which include genes, hormones, physiological structures, or environmental stimuli.	Any phrase by interviews that sheds light on the fighters' physiology and psychology.	Looking into indicators in relevant text and interviews.
	Undesirable traits	Females preferring particular traits in their mates will likely trigger a male with undesirable traits to circumvent a females preference.	Any phrase or statement made by interviewees that referred to fighters having undesirable traits or descriptions, such as the words "savages."	Looking into indicators in relevant text and interviews.

Theory	Concept	Conceptual Definition	Indicators	Assessment
Evolution Theory	Reproduction.	The ultimate benefit from rape is to reproduce.	Any indication or statements made by interviewees that expresses the fighter's intent for forcing pregnancies.	Looking into indicators in relevant text and interviews.
Feminist Rape Theory	The power dimension.	The desire of man to exert dominance over a woman	Any indication or statement made by interviewees that the fighters had a need or urge to feel dominant, such as being forced to perform any task, or being starved, or lack of mercy.	Looking into indicators in relevant text and interviews.
	Gender inequality.	The gender dynamics and sub-ordination of women.	Any indication or statement made by interviewee regarding regarding the level of power balance between captor and captive, especially direct mentions of slavery.	Looking into indicators in relevant text and interviews.

Theory	Concept	Conceptual Definition	Indicators	Assessment
Feminist Rape Theory	Ownership of women.	Women equated to property.	Any indication or statement of slavery or whether there is some sort of ownership structure.	Looking into indicators in relevant text and interviews.
	Sexual objectification.	Females used solely as objects to meet sexual satisfaction.	Indication or statement made by interviewee about how the women were solely used for sexual pleasure.	Looking into indicators in relevant text and interviews
	Spoils of war.	Compensation of war like land and cattle.	Indication made by interviewee that women were given as "gifts" or used as part of a "strategy."	Looking into indicators in relevant text and interviews
	Masculine impotency of the defeated.	Serves as a massive humiliation to the defeated through a blow to their masculinity and honor.	Indication or statement made by interview when the words "shame" and "honor" ar eused with respect to Yezidi men.	Looking into indicators in relevant text and interviews

Theory	Concept	Conceptual Definition	Indicators	Assessment
Feminist Rape Theory	Intimidation and demoralization.	Rape serves as a tactic to intimidate and demoralize the enemy through their women.	Indication or statement that expresses the words of "low morale" or defeat and humiliation.	Looking into indicators in relevant text and interviews.
	Desexualizing rape.	Taking out the sex from the rape and treating it as an act of violence.	Indication or statement made by interviewee mentioning phrases such as "even if they did not want to have sex, they have to do rape in order to perform their duties" or suggestions the crueler they are, the more they are fulfilling their duties.	Looking into indicators in relevant text and interviews.

Theory	Concept	Conceptual Definition	Indicators	Assessment
Feminist Rape Theory	Sexual slavery.	Women are abducted to serve as servants and sexual partners of combatants for extended periods.	Indication of women being used as sex slaves and servants to perform other tasks. Also indication if they knew their rapists.	Looking into indicators in relevant text and interviews.
Strategic Rape Concept	Institutionalization of sexual violence.	Sexual violence is institutionalized such that rape is not random but systematic.	Indication or statement using the words "targeted," "systematic," and/or "planned."	Looking into indicators in relevant text and interviews.
	Ethnic cleansing.	Rape can be used to cleanse an area from a certain ethnic group.	Indication or statements using the words "because Yezdis are not people of the book," "Yezidis are devil worshippers or infidels," or other indications of religious ideology that allowed the targeting of the Yezidis.	Looking into indicators in relevant text and interviews.

Theory	Concept	Conceptual Definition	Indicators	Assessment
Strategic Rape Concept	Collective punishment.	Rape can serve as collective punishment for an ethnic group in conflict.	Indication that all Yezidis are a target by ISIS.	Looking into indicators in relevant text and interviews.
	Reward and compensation.	Rape can serve as an institutionalized means of reward and compensation for combatants.	Indication made by interviewee that women were given as "gifts" or used as part of a "strategy."	Looking into indicators in relevant text and interviews.

Theory	Concept	Conceptual Definition	Indicators	Assessment
Strategic Rape Concept	Strategic rape.	When an organization institutionalized sexual slavery or forced marriage, or purposefully adopted sexual violence in pursuit of the organization's objectives.	Indication or statements made by the interviewee using the words "strategic" or "tactical," or referring to the use of sexual violence to heighten morale and recruitment. Other indications could refer to geopolitical gains.	Looking into indicators in relevant text and interviews.

4.5 Reliability

Reliability refers to the possibility that the study's operations can be repeated and yield the same results.[140] Reliability alone is not enough to prove validity, but they can complement each other. Many techniques were used to attain the data needed for this investigation. These techniques varied from empirical research (using scholarly sources and some media sources) and field interviews. The techniques were employed consistently, though the style of interviews differed from participant to participant due to the context and sensitivity of the topic. This issue remained an on-going problem, for Yezidi women remained enslaved by ISIS during this project. It is thus possible that new information obtained from them at a later time could yield different answers.

4.6 Internal Validity and External Validity

Internal validity for this research is high as there was an in-depth examination via the use of different sources. Even though there were limitations, which will be further addressed in the section below, this case still lacks information as this particular part of history is still being written. Further information and research may possibly yield different or similar conclusions.

External validity, on the other hand, refers to how the case study's findings can be generalized. This single-case study's objective is to test theories in order to prove that cases of sexual violence are unique

---

[140] Yin, Robert K. "Designing Case Studies Identifying Your Case(s) and Establishing the Logic of Your Case Study." *Case Study Research and Applications: Design and Methods*. 6th ed. Los Angeles, CA: SAGE, 2018. 24-80. Print.

and one finding cannot be applied to all cases. The findings of this research are limited to the case of ISIS's use of sexual violence against the Yezidi women because each act of sexual violence varies. Generalizing the findings of this case may be imprudent.

4.7 Limitations of the Study

There are some limitations to this study. It is worth reiterating that this subject is on-going in a challenging and volatile region for both researchers and women. It was quite impossible to access to ISIS fighters, so most information comes from one side of the conflict. This led me to rely on the perception of victims and others involved rather than perpetrators or other ISIS informants. The security situation was unstable when I arrived in August 2016. The Iraqi Army's offensive to free Mosul and its surrounding areas had just begun, and there was a lot of tension between the Iraqis and the local Kurdish forces, who both also expected retaliatory attacks from ISIS. As a result, my time in northern Iraq was limited to three weeks. Although I am fluent in Arabic, northern Iraq is predominantly Kurdish, so I had to rely on a translator for two of my interviews.

In order to analyze ISIS's use of sexual violence, a detailed theological discourse would have been an added value, but it would have fallen beyond the scope and length of this study, and, to be fair, it would have deserved a study of its own. One of the most challenging tasks in this research was the operationalization of the concepts. This was a challenge because it is very difficult to define a concept that is very vague, such as sexual desire, and then operationalize it by setting indicators for such vague concepts. The second step was coding the data, which was unstructured because the interviews were mostly conversational due to the heightened sensitivity of the topic. For example, in order to operationalize shoe size, the indicator would be measurement by "inch" or "centimeter," but a concept like trust or sexual desire is very difficult to operationalize because it is very vague. I had to operationalize within the best of my abilities. In Chapter Six, it is hoped, structured questions make this operationalization easier to understand.

Although there were some limitations, I did nevertheless go to Iraq during an active conflict with genocidal elements and was able to gain access to many people directly involved. The fact that I was able to obtain so much information in such circumstances might reasonable outweigh the limitations.

4.8 Ethical and Safety Considerations

This project's aim is to test the theories elaborated above in order to explain ISIS's use of sexual violence. It was, therefore, of great importance to interview the victims who escaped. This decision was not taken lightly because it meant that some of the victims would have to relive the horrors they experienced. I studied guidelines set by the International Red Cross and documents published by the Office of the United Nations High Commissioner for Human Rights (OHCHR). They mostly are similar with respect to approach. Both documents mention that the researcher must brief the interpreter on the sensitivity of the topic, and suggest that the interpreter be selected from trained NGO employees.

The guidelines further stipulate that the researcher must always think in terms of safety and protection of the persons being interviewed by mapping out in advance organizations that can help victims who need assistance.[141] Further, "the investigation plan should include principles and procedures concerning the capture, storage, management, confidentiality and disclosure of information and evidence."[142] Although I extensively studied the guidelines, researching sexual violence in conflict is very challenging, and it is paramount to grasp the sensitive nature of the topic. Before each interview, I had to disclose what the research is about and what it was for, as the victims had grown antagonistic towards journalists. I also had to assure the interviewees that their identities would be protected, that only and my thesis supervisor and myself would know their identities and hear the recordings. Such measures were important to safeguard the interviewee's identity and the success of the research. Additionally, each interviewee was also told that he or she had the right to terminate the interview if necessary.[143] An important yet easily committed mistake is to become too friendly with the interviewee. Although seemingly harmless at first, when both the researcher and interviewee are exposed to trauma or, in the researcher's case, secondary trauma, it is important to detach after each interview. I made this "rooky" mistake with one of my interviewees, and this led me to stop that particular interview in order not to lose objectivity.[144]

---

[141] Bernard, Vincent, Mariya Nikolova, Elvina Pothelet, and Jamie A. Williamson, eds. "Sexual Violence in Armed Conflict." *International Review of the Red Cross- Humanitarian Debate: Law, Police, Action* 96.894 (2014): 427-655. Print.

[142] "Guidelines for Investigating Conflict-Related Sexual and Gender-based Violence Against Men and Boys." *Institute for International Criminal Investigations*. Institute for International Criminal Investigations, 29 Feb. 2016. Web. 05 Aug. 2018.

[143] The verbal agreement is available in the transcripts

[144] That interviewee became a good friend and her help was immense with the other victims.

In addition to ensuring anonymity, confidentiality, and informed consent, other potential ethical dilemmas should be taken into consideration when conducting fieldwork, such as covert research and the involvement with illegal behavior. [145] Fortunately, none of those issues arose.

As for safety, prior to traveling to Iraq, I informed the Dutch consulate that I would be conducting interviews there. I also had to declare to my university that I would be taking this trip at my own risk. My movements were meant to be limited to Irbil, however due to regional tensions most of the interviewees were scattered, and I had no choice but to leave my location and cover Dohuk, Dibaga, Bashiq, and Solaimani. Since I am no stranger to the Middle East, I made sure I had the right protection at all times when entering any IDP camp, and that my accommodation was as safe as possible. However, it is important to note that safety always came first, as was the case in Bashiq, where I had to cut an interview short due to a potential escalation of hostilities as Bashiq was liberated and officially became the front line while I was there. Just forty-five minutes after I arrived, there was increased military activity and I had to return to Irbil. Another risky visit was to the Debaga Camp, where rumors held that ISIS fighters had infiltrated the camp. I could only stay for two hours.

---

[145] Neuman, W. Lawrence. "Field Research and Focus Group Research." *Social Research Methods: Qualitative and Quantitative Approaches: Pearson New International Edition*. Harlow: Pearson Education Limited, 2014. 431-76. Print.

Chapter 5:
Findings

This chapter presents the findings of the study in a narrative form in the style of a journal. This approach captured how I conducted my fieldwork in context. I used the secondary data derived from this research as a type of fact-checking tool, and in some instances as a supporting tool in this narrative. The narrative was based on fourteen interviews, a majority of which were conducted in the field.

5.1 The Narrative

I arrived in northern Iraq around noontime on August 8, 2016. I had a vague picture of what the situation was like but I did not expect it to be this dire. During my first two hours in the country, I visited the Debaga camp, which is about two hours away from Irbil. The camp accommodates 1,000 people, but the camp was filled with 3,000 IDPs. It was so overcrowded that people slept on the floor. I went there because it was important to see the effects ISIS had on non-Yezidis. The camp is refuge mostly to Sunni Iraqis who fled ISIS from villages and cities like Ba'aj, Mosul, and Ramadi. When I first arrived, some people were a little bit nervous; they certainly don't like journalists, as their stories were constantly exploited. However, the children were very curious and a few came to me and asked if I could take pictures of them. I asked them to ask their parents, and that is how a conversation began with the women of the camp. Two women in particular were very sweet and forthcoming and explained to me why the women were scared. They were scared because they feared that I was a journalist and that I would use their names and faces in a story and lead ISIS to them, or worse, trigger ISIS into killing their loved ones that were left behind. I assured them I was

only a student researching ISIS and that I would not be using my findings for any media outlet except for research. I then assured them that their names would be changed, and that there would be no pictures of them. The audios would only be privy to myself and my supervisor. When I explained the concept to them, some women were still scared because they feared that ISIS had already infiltrated the camp and was watching anyone who spoke to journalists or social workers about what life under ISIS was like. So the two ladies, out of a group of ten, were the only people who agreed to speak to me. As I sat down with Miriam and Souraya (aliases), both were very frail and restless. I tried to begin with my prepared questions, but they were already too scared to speak. In fact, out of the ten women with whom I informally spoke when I arrived at the camp, only two agreed to speak to me about their lives under ISIS. I had to take them to the camp director's office so that they could speak freely without anyone else observing them. Miriam was new to the camp; she had lived under ISIS for almost three years. She was more angry than sad and told me how her brother-in-law's arm was cut off because he was accused of stealing.[146] Souraya was nodding along with her as she lost family members to arbitrary executions in Ramadi. They both expressed how they did not want to return to their homes and that we (the West) should bomb their towns to get rid of ISIS. They expressed their belief that ISIS are not real Muslims and observed that there were many foreigners with them.[147] I later asked them if they were sexually assaulted by ISIS fighters, or if anyone in their town was violated, and they both answered me that while none of them had been sexually violated, Yezidi women had been.

Debaga camp was a sobering and overwhelming experience. I saw so many displaced people in a confined area with very few facilities to get them through what seemed like an indefinite transitional period. Some of the IDPs even expressed how the Kurdistan Regional Government (KRG) is making life hard in these camps on purpose in order to filter out ISIS sympathizers. In other words, some IDPs believe there is a war of attrition in the camp due to fears of ISIS already being there. Women in the camp even set up their own watch to report

---

[146] Miriam interview #1
[147] Picture taken at the Debaga Camp, August 2016

suspicious people who may support ISIS. This experience painted the reality of what was happening in Iraq and how there is an acceptance of the fact that sexual violence is only used against the Yezidis. In other words, the Yezidis are specifically targeted.

I later interviewed Yezidi activists and experts who are directly

involved with the Yezidi issue. I realized that even though ISIS claims that they are doing their so-called religious "duty" by cleansing the whole region or infidels or, in the Yezidis' case "devil worshippers," the motivation for their brutality against the Yezidi women seemed to be much more than merely religious. Hussam Salim, director of the Yezidi Organization for Documentation, explained to me that ISIS is not sexually enslaving women out of their ideology alone, but because it is part of their strategy to recruit fighters and deter opponents, among other strategic reasons. I asked Hussam about the victims' ages and he replied to me that there were victims as young as eight years old and as old as seventy who had been raped by ISIS. It was obviously very difficult for

Hussam and his colleague to talk about the youngest victims whom they had interviewed, so I changed the topic back to the sorting process of the women and girls. They explained that the girls given as gifts to high-ranking ISIS officials were the prettiest, and aged fifteen or sixteen. Hussam mentioned that it was a type of standard that they abide by once they sort the girls. After the prettiest were taken as gifts, the rest of the women were sorted into different categories to be sold. They were sold in real slave markets within the ISIS territories and also on the internet. Hussam further explained that the girls were photographed and advertised as virgins, married, a mother with children, etc., and that the prices differed accordingly.

Hussam also mentioned how some of the girls reported gang rape: "More than one man (more than twenty men) raped the same woman in the same night."[148] ISIL's torture methods also included starvation in order to make the women submit. They would deprive them of food or water for days in extreme weather conditions. Another method of making the women submit was sometimes by drugging them.

I asked Hussam how this violence could be explained, specifically why is sexual violence being used by ISIS. Hussam referred to *Dabiq*'s fourth issue, in which ISIS claimed that the Yezidis should be enslaved because they are "devil worshippers" and justified the sexual enslavement of Yezidi women and the killing of Yezidi men. Hussam expressed the opinion that ISIS is so brutal because it wants to scare people. Other witnesses claimed that some Christian and Shabakshi girls were also taken into sexual slavery, but that these were few in number compared to the 5,000-6,000 Yezidi women and girls who were taken.

---

[148] Interview #2 Hussam Salim

When I asked Hussam about cases of pregnancy, he informed me that even though the information is limited it is something they often consider. He mentioned that there have been cases, but that few have been reported. He also stated that many of the victims were given contraceptives and sometimes taken to hospital for abortions. To gain a better understanding of the power dynamic and ownership structure involved, I asked Hussam to elaborate on these elements. He said that the women were mostly slaves and the property of ISIS fighters. He also documented a case in Raqqa, where one of the victims was forced to work on a farm as well in hotel as a maid.

These statements intrigued me as it did not seem that sex was the sole purpose of ISIS enslavement. I asked if he had heard of other cases in which slaves were used to support other ISIS operations. He informed me that he had encountered elderly women who were forced to dig shelters beneath the homes of the fighters where they could avoid coalition airstrikes. In order to learn more about the fighters themselves, I asked Hussam where the fighters were from and also where the women were being sold. His response showed a truly international operation, with many of the fighters coming from all over the world, often to participate in acts of sexual violence and adventurism. He also stated that women were sold not just within the Islamic State, but elsewhere, including the Caucasus and other Arab nations. When I asked if any local men were involved in these crimes of sexual violence, he replied that many of the women said that they knew their rapists, especially those who came from nearby villages, and that they were also able to tell from which Arab tribes they hailed. Some knew their names. Hussam explained the concept of *karafa* (blood brother - similar to godfather), which is a sociocultural norm of relations between Yezidis and Arabs that has taken place for centuries. The purpose is to build strong bonds with neighboring Arabs or Kurds for mutual protection. I wanted to understand if these cases are random or systematic and planned. He said that many of the cases are very similar, and that the process of distributing and selling the women was well organized and orchestrated.

On the same day I interviewed Hussam, I met Rebwar Bilbas from the Women Empowerment Organization in Irbil. I firstly began by asking Rebwar ISIS's reasons for enslaving Yezidi women. He answered that the first was for "pleasure" purposes -- fulfilling sexual desires. He continued that the second reason was to destroy the reputation and the honor of their enemies, and to demoralize them thereby. I pressed further into how sexual enslavement was used as a tactic to demoralize and humiliate, asking him why he believed this was effective. He responded that if you target women and sexually assault them, especially if the group is a minority, their morale is destroyed and subsequently their power to resist is reduced. And indeed, the Yezidi community was devastated. The males within the community were ashamed to talk about the issue as they felt that their honor had been violated. It even made them beg everyone for support and help to reclaim their women from captivity.

To understand ISIS's motives better, I asked Rebwar if he felt these attacks were sexually motivated or violently motivated. His response was that the fighters under their normal and social environment are not usually sexually active as they come from conservative communities that frown upon extramarital sex. They found that using Yezidi women was a good opportunity for them to indulge in sexual pleasure. Rebwar continued that the third reason is political in nature. ISIS was keen to expand its territorial base and that the terror of sexual enslavement disenfranchised the local Sunnis in neighboring regions, who wanted to leverage support for ISIS to marshal resistance against the Shia led Iraqi government that had marginalized them since the regime change in 2003. He noted that when ISIS first arrived in areas such as Mosul and Kirkuk, they were often greeted cheerfully and warmly through the streets, as they were thought to offer salvation from the persecution of the Shia Maliki administration. Fourth, Rebwar claimed that sexual violence used against Yezidi women was also financially motivated, as women who were captured were often sold via multiple transactions, while those fortunate enough to be released were held for large ransom payments. Finally, Rebwar repeated Hussam's observation that the use of Yezidi sex slaves was a way to entice the international recruits.

The next day, I embarked on a journey to Sulaimani, which is one of the main cities in northern Iraq. My first impression was that the city was more developed than Irbil, and somehow more liberal. It has its own airport, a prestigious university, and an impressive infrastructure. Moreover, the Kurds of Sulaimani differed from the Kurds in Irbil, speaking a different dialect of Kurdish, Sorani. The city is, moreover, a PUK stronghold, which is usually known as the leftist, pro-Iranian party that was founded by Kurdish President Jalal Talabani. Upon arrival, I met with a high-ranking PUK official, Sheikh Latif. I began the conversation by first explaining the topic and purpose of my research. Before I had the opportunity to ask any questions explained that ISIS considers the Yezidis to be infidels and that their money, wives, and children are *halal* (legal/kosher) for ISIS adherents to own, and that this is even thought to be their religious duty. Latif went on to explain that a verse in the Koran called "al-Anfal" makes it permissible for a Muslim to loot the money and assault women and to sell the younger girls of infidels. He stated that ISIS relied on these verses and other Prophetic traditions for outlining the treatment of captives taken in military conquest. He states that ISIS believes it is legitimate to kill any man who is over the age of eighteen and to take children as slaves who can be sold. He further told me that "you consider this a crime against humanity, but for them it is part of their religious practices and obligations."[149] I then asked if he believed that ISIS used rape as a strategy to meet their objectives. He responded that ISIS used barbaric practices to frighten their enemies, arguing that they justified this with a Koranic verse stating that "they kill as many as possible and in the most barbaric manner to plant the seeds of fear in the heart of their enemies."[150] Sheikh Latif concluded the interview after speaking about numerous issues, including the Pashmerga's retreat.

Sheikh Latif facilitated my trip to the IDP camp on the outskirts of Sulaimani by granting me access and a security detail to ensure safe passage. He insisted on providing me with this help as he noticed that I was alone and did not expect to meet with a young student, let alone a woman, in this dangerous part of Iraq.

---

[149] Interview #4 Sheikh Latif
[150] Interview #4 Sheikh Latif

When I arrived at the IDP camp, I met with the guards and briefed them on my research. I was anxious, as this was my first interaction with survivors of genocide and I was unsure how I would be

received. I made sure that the security detail stayed outside the tents so as not to make the survivors feel pressured or obliged and better able to talk freely. The first person I spoke to was Nada.[151] Nada was a twenty-five year old Yezidi woman from Sinjar who tried to flee but did not succeed. ISIS captured her and held her and her husband for about seven days. I was relieved that she had a relatively less grim story, which helped me pose the questions without hesitation.

Nada and her husband tried to escape when ISIS first occupied Sinjar. They were caught while fleeing and were taken to a school where they were detained and separated. I asked her if they tried to assault her. She responded by saying that they did try, but that because she was pregnant her condition thwarted the assault since it against ISIS's rules to rape a pregnant woman. They tried to take her to the hospital to abort,

---

[151] Interview #5. Nada is not her real name.

but her husband told her to kill herself if that should happen. Nada and her husband escaped by chance and made it to the IDP camp, where they had lived for two years at the time of the interview. Nada's husband was looking for work to start their lives over again.

I was pleased to hear a story that resulted in some sort of triumph, but I was keen to find if any other women suffered a different fate. I asked Nada if she knew any women from her village who were taken by ISIS. She responded by saying that they were all freed with ransom money and that eighteen of them were there with her in the IDP camp. Unfortunately, I could not ask her more questions, as I was finding the language barrier difficult to overcome. She insisted on speaking Kurdish, and my translator was very frail and had difficulty keeping up with communicating the questions adequately.

After speaking to Nada, I spoke to a young Yezidi man who had lost his entire family. I came to him while he was wrapping up a television interview pleading for information on the whereabouts of his family, whom he had not seen or heard from for two years. Adel,[152] a young man who had not heard from his father and brother in two years, and it was assumed that they had been killed by ISIS forced when they were captured. But he did know that his mother, sister, and sister-in-law were still alive in Mosul, Raqqa, and Tal Afer, and that they are regular sent from place to place. He had received reports that his fifty-year old mother was imprisoned in Badoushm near Mosul, as she was unable to escape. When I asked him to elaborate further on the conditions under which his family had suffered, he was unable to do so as their phones were confiscated and other lines of communication were minimal. It was

---

[152] Interview #6. Adel is an alias.

obvious he was ashamed and hurt to say out loud what has become of his mother, sister, and sister-in-law but his desperation was very clear.

After meeting Adel, I met an old Yezidi couple who asked me not to record them. They asked of me if I was going to Dohuk and asked me to look for their nieces. They had heard that five women out of twenty-three missing family members were able to escape, but that they cannot locate them. They gave me their names and their dates of birth and asked me to look for them. I replied that I will be going to Dohuk and would do my best to find them one way or another. The elderly couple was very sweet as they invited me to their tent and showed me pictures of how their lives were before the genocide. I left the IDP camp back to the PUK headquarters and returned to Irbil that same night.

I met with Krmanj Othman, senior legal advisor of the Independent Commission for Human Rights in Kurdistan, and member of the KRG's Yezidi Genocide Task Force in Irbil. I first asked him whether there was a consistent and deliberate method for the enslavement of Yezidi women. He replied "it is all the same strategy."[153] He explained that when ISIS enters a village, they gather everyone, and then divide them by age, gender, physical fitness/ appearance, etc. Men who declare allegiance to Islam were welcomed and given weapons to join the fight against the Kurdish Peshmerga militia. Those who refused were executed and buried in mass graves. He stated that there are about twenty-seven mass graves in the region. I then asked what happened to the women. He replied that women were divided further by age, marital status, beauty/physical appearance, maternal status (with children, without children, or pregnant). He claimed that generally elderly women

---

[153] Interview #7 Krmanj

were left to die, while those deemed the most beautiful were offered to high-ranking ISIS fighters as slaves.

I asked Othman his views on the motives of this systematic use of violence against Yezidi women. He stated that this is all interconnected, first acknowledging the geopolitical importance of Sinjar as "one of the reasons Yezidis survived is the mountainous structure of the region," where they took refuge in the mountains whenever attacked. The fact this religion survived in the heart of the Islamic world stood out as a success story. He also elaborated on the political complexity of the Yezidis, who are aligned with multiple factions in the region and are also divided among them, including the influence of international powers and local actors in the area, as well as the Sunni-Shia conflict that had been raging over the previous decade.

Second, Othman confirmed that ISIS used sexual violence as means of attracting fighters. He explained that the so-called Islamic State does not have discos and nightclubs where fighters can freely meet women and exercise their desires. Sex slaves are offered as an alternative to satisfy a basic human urge, and that ISIS recognizes that everybody needs it. Othman further stated that Prophetic tradition and *jihad* of Marriage were used to justify these behaviors. I then asked him if he believed that sexual violence against the Yezidis was a military tactic. He stated that it was a means of psychological warfare, not only against the Yezidis but also against the Kurds and the Arabs. The use of sexual violence would frighten people, as it was a direct threat to their honor. He also argued that sexual slavery provided fighters with sex for their wellbeing in periods when they would be fighting for up to fifteen days at a time. I then asked him why Yezidi women in particular are being targeted. Othman maintained that this was because the women of the north are more attractive, purportedly because of the mountainous terrain and its lower availability of oxygen (the lower the oxygen the smaller the nose supposedly becomes).

The third motive Othman identified to explain the use of sexual violence against the Yezidis was monetary. He stated that human trafficking was regularly taking place and that Yezidi women were being sold to countries around the world: "After five years," he speculated, "maybe we will find a Yezidi woman in Saudi with a king." He estimated the income generated by ISIS through the sale of sex slaves: "as an estimation they kidnapped 4,000 women and if they sold half of them each for $10,000 you'd have an estimation" of a total amount of $20,000,000. After providing his views on the motives of why sexual violence was used, I asked if rape was used a means of ethnic cleansing. He replied that if the religious ruling held that it was impermissible to rape Yezidi women, none of them would have been raped. They would have killed them in mass graves along with everyone else. In other words, rape was used for ethnic cleansing as either way they were doomed and specifically targeted. Rape was simply another means of genocidal elimination.

After concluding my interview with Othman, I was invited by Liza Hiddo from the Baghdad Women's Association to attend a Communist Party event in Irbil. The sole purpose of attending the event was to network, and after listening to a lecture on minorities for two hours, I finally got the chance to meet Khidr Domle and other prominent figures who helped my fieldwork in Dohuk.

I left for Dohuk the following day in a taxi. It was a two-and-a-half-hour journey with many roadblocks and checkpoints. I am not new to the concept of checkpoints, and usually a checkpoint means bored soldiers under the burning sun. At the first check point, the taxi driver explained that I do not speak any Arabic and that I am just a student. We managed to get through, but forty-five minutes before reaching Dohuk, a city that is a few kilometers or as the locals would say, one wrong exit away, from Mosul. It is also the main refuge of the surviving Yezidis, which means that it is also heavily guarded. At this Peshmerga checkpoint, I was asked to get out of the car. I was asked to enter a kiosk-like office, where I was interrogated for a whole hour. I was asked where I was from and answered that I am from the Netherlands, but they pointed at my last name asked if I was an Arab. I answered no and explained that my great-great grandfather was probably Arab but claimed that I did not know any Arabic and that I was a student researching the Yezidi genocide. After another thirty minutes of posturing, I remembered that I had my Leiden University ID card with me and asked them to Google Leiden University on their mobile phones. One of the soldiers smiled and told his superior that I was in fact a student and allowed me to pass through. I claimed I did not know any Arabic because if I had showed them that I speak Arabic, that would have been suspicious. My taxi driver told me that they keep an eye on Arabs, especially Syrians trying to get into the Kurdish region to join ISIS.

I finally made it to Yazda, a Yezidi organization that documents and helps Yezidi survivors. My first impression is that it was chaotic and overrun with foreigners who possessed little knowledge of the language, no expertise in trauma, and little knowledge of the region itself.

Thankfully, I made a few friends on my first day. This helped in bypassing some of the unnecessary red tape. I spoke to Ali and Adiba, two young Yezidis who survived the genocide and were then volunteering with Yazda. Upon arrival, I gave Ali and Adiba the names of the girls I was looking for and they started looking for them. After leaving Yazda, I stayed with a French friend who was a former Yazda volunteer with excellent knowledge of the region, as she is a trained historian who has a strong grasp of the language and has been in the region for almost a decade.

After setting myself up in Dohuk, I went to the university and met with Khidr Domle. Domle is a well known Yezidi activist and scholar who lectures at the university. My first question was his views on the goals of ISIS's use of sexual violence. He began by explaining that the Yezidis are seen by ISIS as infidels and non-believers and therefore had to be dealt with according to specific religious texts in the Prophetic traditions, which are controversial among specialists and non-specialists alike.[154] Domle also explained that ISIS's use of sexual violence was intended to elicit the support of local Muslim communities by promising them booty and slaves. He explained that the environment was ripe for this kind of behavior due to high levels of radicalization within these communities. Furthermore, Domle argued that ISIS used this strategy as a warning to their enemies, threatening that they will suffer the same fate as the Yezidis if they fail to join ISIS. Finally, he argued that ISIS used this strategy to fulfill the sexual needs of their leaders and fighters.[155] This was particularly important as many have come from different countries and therefore it also doubled as a recruitment tool.

---

[154] Interview #8 Khidr Domle
[155] Interview #8 Khidr Domle

I then asked Domle why he thought Yezidi women were a prime target. He replied, "I believe that Daesh, by targeting Yezidi women, wanted to deliver a message to the Yezidis that they are infidels and that there is no place for them in this region, so they targeted women aggressively." I asked his opinion of the level of sexual desire displayed by ISIS fighters. He stated that most of the fighters he had dealt with seem to be psychologically ill, as they were obsessed with sex. The survivors also reported how the fighters were "dirty" and how they tried to present themselves as religious but were in fact barbaric and savage in dealing with people, and with women in particular, as they only see women as nothing more than sexual objects. They also viewed women as spoils of war, as slaves and objects of ownership, and they repeatedly and aggressively assaulted them sexually. I asked Domle to elaborate on whether fighters were forcing women to reproduce. He stated that in the beginning they heard of some cases of pregnancies, but that he had not met the victims personally. Abortions are permissible in Yezidi culture, however later in the conflict ISIS stopped caring about pregnancies and the women were given contraceptives.

By this point it was evident a theme was emerging, and I asked Domle to describe the operation in which women were captured. He stated that this operated on three levels. First, was the capture of as many women as possible and their transfer them to different places where ISIS was prepared to handle them. The second stage was to sort the women by characteristics such as age, beauty, marital status, etc. Once sorted, the women were registered and moved around through the Caliphate and beyond. The third point revealed a more organized approach. Domle stated that many testimonies indicated that captives deemed most beautiful were gifted to ISIS leaders. In many cases, these leaders trades these women for financial gain, which can be seen in the picture below where they take pictures of the women and advertised them on the encrypted internet messaging service Telegram via group chats (see picture below).

I then asked Domle if he believed the attacks were ideologically motivated. He stated that most survivors confirmed that before and after every sexual assault, the fighters read verses from Koran in an attempt to show the enslaved women that they are doing something religiously sanctioned. They also forced the woman to dress, eat, and behave in their preferred way. "They refer to them as slaves of the Islamic State." Domle promised to help me find the missing girls and took me around Dohuk and took me to see Thamer Elyass of the Humanity Organization, which assists Yezidi victims.

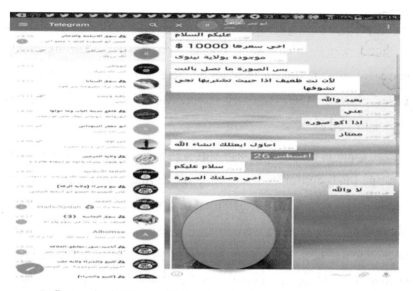

I first asked Elyass if the incidents of rape were random or systematic. He replied that it was systematic and that this was intentional from the beginning. This was legitimized, in ISIS's view, because Yezidis are not "people of the book" and do not believe in God.[156] This allowed the fighters to act with impunity, purportedly following the Koran. "The attack on the Yezidi was planned and they knew they would do it, and they were recruiting people based on [the idea that] there will be slaves for you, free women. It was planned before; it wasn't random."[157] I asked more about whether rape was used as a means of reward or compensation for fighters. Elyass claimed that the strategy as described by the surviving girls was that the youngst and most beautiful ones went to the highest ranking officers. The others were then sold or distributed to the other fighters through slave markets called "Souk al-Nikhasa" ("market of spoils"). He claims that prices were based on physical characteristics. I asked how important were the Yezidis to ISIS

---

[156] Interview #9 Thamer
[157] Interview #9 Thamer

strategically. Elyass explained that in addition to recruitment and gaining local support, which was touched on earlier, Yezidis held a geographically significant location as there is an international road that passes through their territory from Mosul into Syria and from Syria into Turkey.

Later in the evening, as I was walking around Dohuk with Adiba admiring the beautiful landscape of northern Iraq, I got a phone call from Domle, who told me that he had found the women I was looking for. He told me that five of them were in an IDP camp near Dohuk and that the others that had been liberated a few days before and were recovering in a hospital. He told me that I could see them the next day. I was happy that I managed to find them but was also very anxious and nervous. Adiba agreed to come with me, as she herself also narrowly escaped when ISIS captured Sinjar and also knew women from her village. Her presence was thus a familiar one and softened the difficulty of speaking of something so personal and horrific to a total stranger. It is worth mentioning that I felt guilty about asking Adiba to come with me, as the process would burden her with more sadness. She was already documenting survivors for Yazda, which clearly took a toll on her, and on Ali. They were both so young and definitely ill prepared to deal with such heavy burden.

The next day we drove for forty minutes outside Dohuk to the Yezidi IDP camp called Sarya. Sarah's relative who directed me to their makeshift house met Adiba and me. Sarah invited us into their living room with her two-year-old son, great aunt, and four cousins. They all have one thing in common; each person in that room had been an ISIS sex slave and managed to escape, including Sarah's great aunt, who was eighty years old. It was a chilling moment at first because I certainly did not expect so many people. Nevertheless, I asked them if they would like to talk to me at the same time, and they all agreed that they would much rather do so together rather than speak separately.

I noticed that the great aunt was holding on to pictures and was very quiet and sad. The cousins were trying to be hospitable but were definitely shaken up. Sarah was the most outspoken one with a strong presence. She insisted on making me tea and offered me some pastries. Sarah was twenty-five and had only been married for a year when she was captured. Her son was only a few months old at the time. She explained how they were all captured as they were trying to flee. She told me that "we were about twenty people and we left the house, and *Daesh* [ISIS] caught us. They killed the men and took the women. They took us to Ba'aj and then to Mosul."[158] Sarah continued, "they left us in a school [in Ba'aj], the men in one room and us women in another. We had in mind that they only caught us, but there were many other women. Two hours later, they brought nine trucks." The "trucks" were big tourist buses. The buses took them to Mosul to the Galaxy Hall, where they stayed for ten days, and this is when they found out that they were slaves.

Sarah explained that all the women and girls were taken, starting from age nine. They were then sorted by age, up to women over age twenty. Their captors then took them to a house and left them there as each fighter came to choose one. Whoever resisted was brutally beaten. Sarah claimed that if a woman did not rise when summoned, she would be dragged forward by her hair. Their captors forced them to shower and threatened them with more beatings. After two days at the house, Sarah

---

[158] Interview #10 Sarah

was raped, along with her friend, and after that she was sent to another house.

During Sarah's narrative, her cousins were nodding along and told me that they went through the same ordeal. My facial expressions began to change involuntarily as hearing such stories firsthand is nothing like reading about it. Sarah noticed my facial expressions changing and told me "hey, this out fate – it's ok; I am ok." She did not let me see her as a victim even once during our three conversations. She further explained how her captors told her that her husband was dead, though he was not, and how the fighter was yelling at her and threatening to take her son if she did not submit.

After two months of imprisonment, Sarah, her friend, and her cousins tried to escape to a house in Mosul, but the owner of the house reported all six of them. They were taken by ISIS and, in the extreme heat, were locked in a bathroom without any milk for her infant son. Sarah's cousin told me that her son was traumatized by the horrendous first two years of his life. After being locked in the bathroom for three hours, each man took one of the women and took their children away to the garden. They brought back six cables and began beating all six women. Sarah still bears the marks of the beating and suffers from her injuries. The next day she was sold to an ISIS fighter who already owned Sarah's friend, which offered her some sort of solace. The fighter threatened to resell her if she refused to sleep with him. She was raped again and a month later she was sold again. This time, she was sent to Ba'aj where she stayed for four months. This man who purchased her took her to see her family in Tal Afar, apparently, as Sarah believed, because he felt sorry for her in some way. Even so, he raped her every night. She mentioned how the fighters justify raping captive women, telling them that it is their right because they are the women are slave. Sarah's family in Tal Afar was spared, however, because they converted to Islam. She, however, was told that she would be taken to Syria.

Sarah was forced to wear the *niqab* with the gloves because she was a slave, but she wore her normal clothes underneath. Her trip to Raqqa began as she was taken onto a big bus in a six-bus convoy carrying 150 women and 500 children. They traveled for two days without food or drink, and the children were crying from hunger. They were then taken to a basement and kept there for five days without any food or water. Her cousin recalls that she was there and how they had to use the washing machine water in order to drink. It got worse when the toilets backed up and the stench became unbearable. They were then transferred to a physics and chemistry institute on the road to Aleppo, where they stayed for seven months. After that, Sarah and her cousin were separated again when they were sold. After searching for each other, they met again and managed to escape from Raqqa. Sarah escaped by stealing the house keys. They then took refuge in the house of a woman who helped arrange their further flight. They walked for nine hours to Kobane, from which they returned to their home region. Sarah took out her phone and showed me pictures of what their lives were like and pictures of the remaining women in the family who were still held by the Islamic State. She was overjoyed when I told her that I had found her aunt and uncle in the IDP camp near Sulaimani. Her cousins were sitting on the room nodding as she was talking, as they all share her story. But the saddest image of them all was that of the eighty-year-old great aunt, who was sobbing over the girls who were still gone. She herself had been taken by ISIS, which was unusual, but after her capture they just left her.

Sarah's and her cousins' stories stayed with me for a very long time. I intuited that there was still more to their stories but did not push for further answers or details. Sarah's speaking to me so freely was brave enough, especially since she had only been back for three months. After we were done with the interview, we moved on to lighter topics, such as my soft Lebanese accented Arabic, which tried to imitate, and about their future plans. I found those women to be strong, as they did not allow me to see them as victims but rather as *survivors*.

On my last day in Dohuk, I was meant to speak with another survivor but due to her distressed mental state I opted to cancel the interview, as I did not want to cause her greater harm. Instead, I interviewed Abdullah, a smuggler. Abdullah, who is from Sinjar, lost fifty-six family members to ISIS and had only been able to release only thirty-two of them. He explained how he got interested by telling me:

> In the beginning I was forced to get into this because of the disinterest [*sic*] of people and countries in our case made us rely on ourselves. In the beginning in 2014, in October, or even three days before then by niece called me from Raqqa and she told me she was in a specific place under *Daesh*. I had to get involved in these things and I took advantage of the relationships I had earlier when I was a trader. I called those merchants and my friends with whom I worked to get involved and rescue these people. In that time, if there were countries or specialised organizations working on these issues, I would have called them directly and not get involved myself or think about it. And up until that moment, September 27, 2014, I had never thought of rescuing. So I had to get involved. So I called my friends and I did not tell them directly that I would be working on this but I told them I needed smugglers for cigarettes because cigarettes are like Yezidis: forbidden with the *Daeshis*. Both of these are forbidden. So I thought to get involved through cigarettes. So they told me those traders I used to work with - they told me you

cannot work in smuggling. But I said yes I work in smuggling. They did not believe that I would work in smuggling goods. I told them there is no more work and I have no choice. The cigarette smugglers from Syria looked for others for me. If they were making a thousand dollars, we gave them two, we always gave them more than they used to make to get them involved in this.[159]

Abdullah had rescued 264 women by the time I met him. ISIS had placed a big price on his head, according to him, but he was

comfortable with letting me use his name after he conducted an interview with the BBC. He further explained to me how he organizes the whole operation by using his phone, or as he put it, "my phone is everything I own and runs everything." He meant that he never crossed the YPG or Peshmerga lines as he used his network of smugglers to get the girls back. He told me how ISIS tried to trap them by forcing the women to call him to arrange a pick up, but thankfully he never fell for it. He recalled how hard it was to listen to a thirteen-year-old survivor relate

---

[159] Interview #11 Abdullah

how she was raped eight times by different fighters and how some women who became pregnant by ISIS fighters committed suicide. He also mentioned how a *fatwa* was issued to let all the Yezidi women know that whether or not they were pregnant, they were welcome to come back and that they should not be ashamed. There were, however, some twenty-one victims who committed suicide because of the stigma. Abdullah later on explained how the operations were planned but asked that I not publish this information as there were more women to be rescued.

After spending a week in Dohuk, I returned to Irbil, where I began consolidating my data. I could not help but realize the striking similarity between stories when I read the *New York Times* article "ISIS Enshrines a Theology of Rape" by Rukmini Callimachi.[160] Callimachi shared survivor stories, which were almost identical to Sarah's and her cousins' stories. For example, all the survivors talked about how they were separated and the how the men were executed. I got goosebumps when I realized that these survivors might have even known Sarah and her cousins as they were all taken to the same "sorting" center. A survivor identified as "F says she was driven to the Iraqi city of Mosul some six hours away, where they herded them into the Galaxy Wedding Hall."[161]

It was my last day and I was still missing one interview, with a general of the Kurdish Peshmerga militia forces. I accompanied two

---

[160] Callimachi, Rukmini. "ISIS Enshrines a Theology of Rape." *The New York Times*. The New York Times, 13 Aug. 2015. Web. 4 Aug. 2018. <https://www. nytimes. com / 2015 / 08 / 14 / world / middleeast /isis - enshrines - a - theology -of-rape.html>.

[161] Callimachi, Rukmini. "ISIS Enshrines a Theology of Rape." *The New York Times*. The New York Times, 13 Aug. 2015. Web. 4 Aug. 2018. <https://www.nytimes.com/2015/08/14/world/middleeast/isis-enshrines-a-theology-of-rape.html>.

volunteer medics to Bashiq in their ambulance, as they know the general very well. I was slightly nervous to go the front line just for an interview, but I downplayed the situation, thinking it would be like the front line in Lebanon, which is relatively safe. As we arrived in Bashiq, General Bahram Areef Yasine and a staff officer greeted me. General Bahram only speaks Kurdish and German, so his officer offered to translate even though I gave the general the option of conducting the interview in German. He gave me a tour of the front line and briefly explained what was going on with respect to the offensive as we heard Turkish tanks operating.

I started the interview by asking General Bahram whether there were any tactical benefits for ISIS to hold Yezidi women and children. He replied that "there are lots of purposes that ISIS does this. The first one is that to spread fear among the people, for example in Mosul, so that they would know there is a strong force, a good force, for ISIS. The second purpose is to use these people as humanitarian wall or like armor."[162] I asked the general to explain more about ISIS's use of Yezidi women and children as human shields. He elaborated:

> ISIS lost a lot of power so when they realize there is an imminent attack from the Peshmerga or that Iraqi forces will attack Mosul, they make sure that the foreign fighters coming from Europe and the US move to Syria. Local ISIS fighters ask if there is an imminent attack, what is the best thing to do? They say the best thing is to use the civilians, women and children and Yezidis, as a human shield and surround ourselves and make sure the Peshmerga does not kill us. We send those families in front of us because Peshmerga will not kill those families. So this is their process and tactic for the future. For the imminent future that will happen.[163]

---

[162] Interview #12 Gen. Bahram
[163] Interview 12 Gen. Bahram

At this point I had to end my interview as the situation was slightly escalating and I had an anxious feeling that I had to leave. We quickly made our way out and back to Irbil.

164

A few months later, I read Nadia Murad's book, *The Last Girl*.[165] Murad chronicles her own abduction by ISIS and how she escaped. Her story was almost identical with respect to how they were taken and how they were sorted and raped.   She recalled, for example, that she was loaded on big tour bus and taken to Mosul, where she was selected and confined to a house where she and her fellow captives were sold.[166] I was also shocked to read Farida Khalaf's *The Girl Who Beat ISIS: My Story*, in which she related how she was taken from her village and assaulted by

---

[164] This was the picture taken with the two American medics, one of whom was a Peshmerga volunteer.
[165] Murad, Nadia. "Chapter 1." *The Last Girl: My Story of Captivity, and My Fight against the Islamic State.* 1st ed. New York: Tim Duggan, Print.
[166] Murad, Nadia. "Chapter 4." *The Last Girl: My Story of Captivity, and My Fight against the Islamic State.* 1st ed. New York: Tim Duggan, 2017. 125-35. Print.

ISIS.[167] Krmanj and Hussam were able to give me a draft of their project, in which they compiled survivors' stories. All twenty cases were identical with respect to how the survivors were captured and how they were sorted and raped.[168]

By this point in my research, I was confident to describe ISIS's attack on the Yezidi women as systematic, planned, and institutionalized. In correspondence with Elizabeth Jean Wood, she replied to an inquiry from me that "it is clearly a POLICY of the organization, so it is not a practice. It is highly REGULATED by the group."[169]

---

[167] Khalaf, Farida, and Andrea C. Hoffmann. "The Catastrophe." *The Girl Who Beat ISIS*. London: Square PEG, 2017. 30-57. Print.
[168] Since this was a draft it will be available upon request.
[169] Correspondence EJW

Chapter 6:
Analysis

6.1 Introduction to Analysis

This chapter presents the explanatory strengths of the theories introduced earlier in the book, the strengths of new factors, and any remaining relevant observations based on the empirical findings. It was evident through all of the interviews that ISIS's use of sexual violence was deliberate and systematic, and not an unfortunate biproduct of war. The testimonials described an industrial-like operation that was complex, well structured, legitimized through Islamic courts, and sometimes even digitized. The findings also showed a multitude of interconnected reasons why sexual violence was used. These can be broadly classified as religious, geopolitical, and strategic, as well as aligned with the core theories of this study. In the next three sections, using the data presented in Chapter Five will test the main three theories.

6.2 Evolution Theory

Randy Thornhill and Craig Palmer linked evolution theory to explaining sexual violence. They stated that men rape due to a biological urge that was passed down from male ancestors.[170] The ultimate reason to rape is to procreate by bypassing the women's right to accept or veto intercourse due to the male's fear that their appearance might not help them in procreating in order to preserve their bloodline.[171]

1- What is the level of sexual desire displayed by the ISIS fighters?

When I asked this question, there was a general consensus that the Yezidi women were being used as objects of sexual pleasure. A regular explanation is that the repressive societies from which most ISIS fighters originate causes them to have an increased sexual desire, as sex is not readily available or permissible and is religiously frowned upon. In an interview with Khidr Domle, he noted of ISIS fighters: "most of those I have dealt with they seem to be psychological ill. They are thirsty for sex." Krmanj Othman also tried to explain this desire for sex by stating that fighters have a high sex drive due to going for long period on the front line and that it is also human nature. He also stated that the level sexual desire is high because Yezidi women are considered attractive. Thamer Elyass stated that victims he interviewed regularly reported that fighters "repeatedly and aggressively assaulted them regularly" and "only see women as sexual objects and no more."

These observations could infer that the fighters had high levels of sexual desire as they viewed women only as sex objects. When I asked the victims firsthand about the frequency of assault, they replied that rape was a constant factor in their captivity, thus implying that their captors'

---

[170] Thornhill, Randy, and Craig Palmer. *A Natural History of Rape: Biological Bases of Sexual Coercion.* Cambridge, MA: MIT, 2001. Print.
[171] Thornhill, Randy, and Craig Palmer. *A Natural History of Rape: Biological Bases of Sexual Coercion.* Cambridge, MA: MIT, 2001. Print.

sexual desire was high. Moreover, in some cases it was reported that fighters took more than one woman as sex slaves, which could imply an even higher level of sexual desire. Furthermore, this argument could be supported, as was evident from the research, by the observation that ISIS used the promise of sex slaves as a principal recruitment method.[172] ISIS was able to tap into this psyche and use it for its own gains.

2- Are there any clear proximate causes that can be attributed to incidents of rape?

It was challenging to determine whether there were any proximate causes, as I did not have access to ISIS fighters or any direct information about biological proximate causes. However, it could be argued that long periods on the front line are likely to increase sexual desire, and hence the incidence of rape. Krmanj Othman noted that fighters could be on the front line for weeks, which increased their sex drive. A secondary report has shown, furthermore, that ISIS "members from Europe and the US found that a cohort had a history of domestic and sexual violence,"[173] preexisting factors "suggesting a relationship between committing terrorist attacks and having a history of physical and/or sexual violence."[174] For example, both the Westminster and Nice attackers had histories of violence and domestic abuse.[175]

---

[172] 90% of interviewees mentioned that sex slaves were used a recruitment tool.
[173] Townsend, Mark. "Rape and Slavery Was Lure for UK Isis Recruits with History of Sexual Violence." *The Guardian*. Guardian News and Media, 07 Oct. 2017. Web. 05 Aug. 2018.
[174] Malik, Nikita. *Trafficking Terror: How Modern Slavery and Sexual Violence Fund Terrorism*. Publication. London: Henry Jackson Society, 2017. Print.
[175] Malik, Nikita. *Trafficking Terror: How Modern Slavery and Sexual Violence Fund Terrorism*. Publication. London: Henry Jackson Society, 2017. Print.

3- What are the undesirable traits displayed by ISIS fighters?

As it was not possible to gain access to ISIS fighters, it was difficult to know firsthand about their undesirable traits. Moreover, due to the ethical need to safeguard the emotional wellbeing of the survivors, I did not ask probing question about their attackers themselves in order not to trigger more trauma. Hence, through anecdotal evidence I have gathered that the fighters were portrayed as unattractive, dirty, "savage," and "barbaric."

4- Were ISIS fighters forcing women to reproduce?

In my interview with Hussam, he revealed that very few cases of pregnancies have been reported and that information is limited due the social stigma and shame regardless of religious edicts intended to support survivors and facilitate their return to their communities. He also stated that ISIS offered contraceptives and abortions to the victims. Furthermore, Khidr Domle stated that in the beginning they heard of a few cases of pregnancies, however he had not encountered them personally. He explained that this could be because Yezidis allow abortions. He also stated, however, that "later *Daesh* didn't care about pregnancy. They gave pills, medicine and injections against pregnancies." Finally, the victims said that they had not seen any cases of pregnancy. Abdullah the smuggler mentioned that he was aware of cases of pregnancy, but that the victims committed suicide due to the social stigma.

According to Nadia Murad, a survivor of the genocide, ISIS did not enforce pregnancy on Yezidi women because their rules forbid pregnant women from being traded, sold, or assaulted, this implies that a pregnancy sex slaves is a loss for the slave owner which is one of the reasons why they administer contraceptives and offer abortions.[176]

5- What were the ages of the women who were targeted?

It is evident from the interviews that the ages of the women captured ranged significantly, from as young as eight to as old as seventy. Some of the younger girls were often gifted to ISIS leaders, as mentioned by the majority of the interviewees. Abdullah the smuggler informed me that he rescued a young girl aged thirteen who was "married" to eight people during her captivity, which lasted less than a year. It seems that the sole purpose of sexual violence was not to impregnate women, for some victims were below or above child bearing age. I interviewed a frail seventy-year-old woman who was assaulted by ISIS. Adel's mother was fifty years old and was taken by ISIS as a slave. Yet in some instances, such as in Nadia Murad's story, older women were killed or abandoned by ISIS because they was much older.

Discussion:

Elements of evolution theory apply to ISIS. These include the innate sexual desire and undesirable characteristics of the male fighters.[177] However, evolution theory argues that the sole purpose of rape is to procreate,[178] and from the evidence it seems that this was generally not the case. It is challenging to draw definitive conclusions from the evidence, as there is a lack of empirical data to support these

---

[176] Murad, Nadia. "Chapter 4." *The Last Girl: My Story of Captivity, and My Fight against the Islamic State.* 1st ed. New York: Tim Duggan, 2017. 125-35. Print.

[177] Thornhill, Randy, and Craig Palmer. *A Natural History of Rape: Biological Bases of Sexual Coercion.* Cambridge, MA: MIT, 2001. Print.

[178] Thornhill, Randy, and Craig Palmer. *A Natural History of Rape: Biological Bases of Sexual Coercion.* Cambridge, MA: MIT, 2001. Print.

claims as well as access to the fighters themselves. Proximate causes do seem visible but not explicit. Moreover, it is important to note that evolution theory does not consider context, which is problematic as context is extremely important to this case study.

6.3 Feminist Theory

Feminist theory focuses on the power dimension -- why women are subordinated and violated, particularly in conflict situations.[179]

1- How were fighters exerting dominance over their victims?

It is evident from all of the interviews that ISIS was exerting dominance over its victims. This took place through numerous forms, namely, by killing the victims' families, starving them, beating them, sexually enslaving them, forcefully moving them, and forcefully converting them. In his interview, Thamer Elyass wondered "what mercy could be done a to a slave?" Khidr Domle stated that the fighters were barbaric and savage when dealing with women. The victims recounted that they were starved for days in extreme weather conditions and how their newborns' safety was threatened to force them to submit to sex. ISIS would also sometimes tell them that their husbands and other male family members had been killed in order to break their spirits and force them to submit. If one of the women tried to resist, they would bring them all of out and beat them until they submitted. One the victims told me, "they beat us in these houses. We wouldn't move from our places, so they would beat us. And if a woman doesn't get up they would

---

[179] Brownmiller, Susan. "War." *Against Our Will: Men, Women and Rape.* New York: Ballantine, 1993. 31-113. Print.

hold her from her hair and drag her up the stairs." She also told me that failure to accept rape resulted in beatings.

2- What was the balance of power between captor and captive?

The balance of power was clear. The captives were slaves, property of the Islamic State, in which their human rights were non-existent and they were often forced to do many things against their will. Domle stated that ISIS fighters forced the women to dress, eat, and behave as they willed, a practice confirmed by Murad's book. The lives of the women were in the hands of the fighters at all times and therefore ISIS had total control over them.

3- What was the ownership structure?

In all cases the women were enslaved, meaning that the ownership structure was straightforward. They were considered and treated as property. Nevertheless, the conditions of enslavement followed Islamic law as interpreted by ISIS. For example, when a fighter died, his slaves became free. Domle mentioned, however, that this law was overruled in practice and that captive women were sold all over again.

4- What were the main uses of Yezidi women for ISIS?

The research shows that sexual slavery was not always the only use of the Yezidi women. In other cases they were used for different purposes, such as digging tunnels, farming, and domestic service. Although some of the day-to-day uses varied, the one thing these cases had in common is that many women – especially younger women -- were used exclusively as sex slaves. Hussam stated that he had documented cases in Raqqa in which women were bought and sold as slaves to work on farms but that these tended to be the older women, who were not raped. Other than being slaves, women were also used as a commodity such as a gift.

5- Were the victims used as spoils of war to compensate fighters?

As previously mentioned, many of the younger and more attractive girls were gifted to the high-ranking ISIS leaders. Nearly all of the interviews mention how the prettiest girls were gifted and marketed on social media, while the rest were sold in slave markets. ISIS fighters had chat rooms on Telegram, an internet messaging service, in which they would send pictures of the women and try and sell them. They were also sometimes perverse social exchanges in which slaveowners shared their slaves with other men. It was clear that captive women and girls were used as commodities, and in some cases currency, by the Islamic State. However, since many of the women were bought, they cannot always be considered "compensation."

6- Were the fighters humiliating the defeated men?

It was evident that the remaining surviving Yezidi men were demoralized as they felt that their honor has been violated. Rebwar Bilbas stated that "the Yezidi community after this was devastated. They couldn't go and say that. I mean that they were very ashamed to say in the Yezidi community that their honor was already lost." Domle, a Yezidi himself, also shared this view and claims how this humiliated the men of the community. ISIS even told the women in the beginning of their captivity that they could call their families and tell them they are now slaves and that this is their punishment for being infidels, non-believers, and non-Muslims". The fact they allowed them to communicate with their remaining family members in this way shows that they were trying to humiliate the defeated men. This ultimately suppressed their ability to resist, an intentional consequence.

7- How effective was rape as an intimidation and demoralization tactic?

It is evident that rape was intended to strike fear in the hearts of ISIS's enemies and break their morale through a grotesque display of slavery, torture, and sexual violence against something that is held most precious to their communities. The Yezidis are known to be a proud people who live according to a strict code of honor and dignity, which was completely degraded by ISIS. The research shows that this is a clear form of psychological warfare, which often had the desired effect not just on the Yezidis but on the region as a whole and, arguably, throughout the word. This is evident from the quick gains made by ISIS as a result of armed forces and civilians fleeing even before heavy clashes had begun. Hamza al Ansari, a senior ISIS figure, was quoted as saying in the early stages of the war, "We'll conquer and enslave your women and turn your children to orphans."

8- To what extent was the rape sexually motivated or violently motivated?

The safe answer would be both, since the reports tell us that even when the fighters do not want to have sex, they say that they have to have sex because they believe it to be their religious duty. This can explain why rape was in some cases "officiated" with prayers before and after the act. Moreover, as many interviewees reported, the act of rape was violent in itself, which means that it could be possible that rape was both sexual and violent. For example, Sarah stated, "slavery doesn't happen without rape." Domle, moreover, noted that the fighters repeatedly and aggressively assaulted the victims sexually.

9- Were women abducted as servants and forced to be sexual partners of combatants?

It was evident from all of the interviews that the primary reason for abduction was for sexual slavery, as all of the victims and reports have reported sexual assault. However, in some cases the women were also used as servants, as Hussam has pointed out that some of the women till the land as slaves, particularly older women who were put to work in hotels or farms.

10- Were the perpetrators anonymous to the victims?

As pointed out by Hussam and other interviewees, the victims knew their rapists in many instances due to the strong relationships between their communities and the neighboring Arab communities.

Discussion:

It is clear that many elements of feminist theory apply to the case study, but elements such as the anonymity of the perpetrator and de-sexualization of the act of rape do not entirely resonate with the theory. According to feminist theory, the reason why men rape is connected to anonymity, but many of the victims here knew their attackers.[180] Also, according to feminist theory, men will rape women if given the chance,[181] but here that is not the case, as only non-pregnant Yezidis were targeted. Moreover, it is difficult to de-sexualize the act of rape in this case since there a high level of sexual desire was expressed.

---

[180] Brownmiller, Susan. "War." *Against Our Will: Men, Women and Rape.* New York: Ballantine, 1993. 31-113. Print.
[181] Brownmiller, Susan. "War." *Against Our Will: Men, Women and Rape.* New York: Ballantine, 1993. 31-113. Print.

6.4 Strategic Rape Concept

Strategic rape concept refers to the use of sexual violence in conflict as a means of achieving military objectives and thus constituting another weapon of war.[182]

1- Were the incidents of rape random or systematic?

It was evident that ISIS's use of sexual violence was systematic. Many of the interviewees described an identical process for the capture and distribution of women, which clearly showed intent. Hussam explained that many of the girls whom he had encountered had informed him of the distribution process was intentional, well planned, and not random. In other words, the systematic use if rape occurred as follows:

i. When ISIS entered a village, the men, women, and children were rounded up and invited to convert to Islam. If they did, they would be welcomed and given arms to join the fight. The men who refused were normally rounded up and executed in mass graves.

ii. Once the men had been executed, ISIS sorted the women and children by a range of characteristics, e.g. age, marital status, physical appearance, etc. The weak and elderly women were often left to die while girls as young as eight were sent to different distribution centers, where they were ultimately gifted or sold as slaves to ISIS leaders, fighters, and supporters. It was widely reported that those deemed to be more beautiful were gifted to leaders as spoils of war and those that were being sold commanded a higher premium based on age, beauty, and other desirable characteristics.

---

[182] Barstow, Anne Llewellyn. "Introduction." *War's Dirty Secret: Rape, Prostitution, and Other Crimes against Women.* Ed. Anne Llewellyn. Barstow. Cleveland, OH: Pilgrim, 2000. 1-10. Print.

iii. Girls and women were distributed and sold via a sophisticated network of markets, agents and even online platforms, highlighting the technological advancements of the human trafficking trade.

iv. Once sold as slaves to serve in farms, hotels, or households, girls and women were subjugated, forced to wear the *niqab*, and regularly beaten and abused by their captors, who in all reported cases regularly sexually violated them. Starvation and blackmail were often the preferred use of persuasion, but direct death threats or threats to children and other family members were not uncommon. The interviews also showed that in some cases multiple people raped the victims collectively.

v. It was not uncommon for several transactions and relocations to take place throughout the Caliphate, with some girls and women reported to have been held as slaves under numerous owners.

2- To what extent was rape used as a means of ethnic cleansing?

The research shows that rape was also used as a method of ethnic cleansing since ISIS institutionalized sexual slavery as a policy due to the Yezidis' ethnicity and religion. Krmanj Othman mentioned how the Yezidi women could have either ended up dead or as sex slaves; in other words, they were ethnically cleansed in a different way. Yezidi men were also massacred if they refused to convert to Islam. Domle quoted Abu Hamzah Al Ansari, a senior ISIS figure, who reportedly stated in the early stages the war, "we came to exterminate you. We will conquer you and enslave your women and make your children orphans."

3- Was rape used as a form of collective punishment for the Yezidis?

As previously mentioned, the Yezidis were targeted because ISIS considers them to be "devil worshippers." Because they are not Muslims and do not belong to an Abrahamic faith, the Yezidis were subject to genocidal persecution. As Domle stated, "Yezidis are seen [by ISIS] as infidels and nonbelievers and have to be punished this way." When Sarah confronted her captor and challenged his behavior as un-Islamic, he responded, "You are an infidel, why should I help you?"

4- Was rape used as a means of reward or compensation for combatants?

It was reported by almost all interviewees that the prettiest girls were often gifted to the most senior ISIS leaders. It is important to note that not all owners of sex slaves acquired them by means of compensation, as they had to pay for their slaves, which is not a form of compensation.

5- How did ISIS use rape to meet its strategic objectives?

It is evident that rape was intended to strike fear in the heart of ISIS's enemies and to break their moral through a grotesque display of slavery, torture, and sexual violence in order to weaken resistance. The research shows that this is a clear form of psychological warfare that often had the desired effect, not just on the Yezidis, but on the region as a whole. This is evident from the quick gains made by ISIS as a result of armed forces and civilians fleeing even before heavy clashes begun. Hamza Al Ansari, a senior ISIS figure, was quoted as saying in the early stages of the war "We'll conquer and enslave your women and turn your children to orphans," demonstrating that the use of rape was a premeditated tactic carefully designed to instill terror. The research also revealed that captives were regularly allowed to call their families, likely so that they could let them know the horrors they faced and thereby spread the contagion of fear.

Recruitment Tool – ISIS's advanced global recruitment campaign has been widely documented in the media and academia, but it is evident from this research that the promise of sex slaves was also a primary recruitment tool to attract supporters and fighters from the region and around the world. As part of this sophisticated strategy, social media platforms such as You Tube and the encrypted communications platform Telegram showed images of Yezidi women for sale and being sold. The research shows that those who came into contact with ISIS fighters regularly questioned their mental states, moral limits, and extreme sexual appetites.

Human Shields – By interviewing a general in the anti-ISIS Kurdish Peshmerga forces, it was evident that ISIS was using sex slaves as a means of defense, including as human shields. This was particularly the case when ISIS began losing ground and faced heavy land and air assaults by coalition forces. It was argued that this was a desperate last-ditch attempt to stop opposition forces from advancing on their positions due to fear of civilian casualties.

Morale Boost – Not only did the promise of sex slaves attract fighters, but it was also seen as a way of enhancing their morale and ultimately their performance in battle. This can be demonstrated by the gifting of the younger and more beautiful girls to senior fighters as a spoil of war and booty to reward their commitment to the cause.

Economic - The research shows that ISIS's use of sexual violence also has a strong financial motive, evident from the human trafficking enterprise that was established and run with corporate efficiency. Women were regularly sold through numerous transactions throughout the Caliphate and beyond, providing a substantial source of income. The use of registration and distribution centers throughout the region, serviced via fleets of vans and buses to transport the victims, shows the operational complexity. The establishment of slave markets and online trading platforms further demonstrated this motive as they facilitated the sale of sex slaves with great efficiency. The use of these forums provided ISIS with a viable channel of revenue generation to support war efforts. Further, the research shows that ISIS resorted to extortion and blackmail through the use of substantial ransom fees, which reportedly ranged between $10,000 - $20,000 dollars per person. Despite the lack of availability of accurate figures, a crude estimate based on interview data is that this source could have generated between $20,000,000 dollars or more in ransom money alone. Although Yezidis are generally rural and poor, the research found that the Kurdish Regional Government was in some cases reimbursing families who had evidence of their kidnapping but would rarely cover the costs up front.

Strategic: In addition to luring recruits, four of the interviewees -- Krmanj, Rebwar, Hussam, and Thamer – identified the region around Sinjar as a strategically important mountainous area that connects Mosul to Raqqa. Therefore, one of ISIS's main strategic objectives was to displace all the inhabitants from Sinjar in order to establish an unhindered supply route between the Caliphates main centers of power.

6- Did the Yezedi victims know their rapists?

As previously mentioned in feminist theory, the victims often knew their rapists.

Discussion:

It is evident that almost all the elements of strategic rape concept apply to this case study. However, even though the Yezidi women did know their rapists in some instances, ISIS had many foreign fighters, and victims have mentioned being enslaved by foreigners. In at least some cases, therefore, the fighters did not solely rape the women due to familiarity.[183] Another element that does not entire apply is that fact that some victims were solely given as a form of reward or compensation. As mentioned before, not all women were given as gifts as they were sold and bought on numerous occasions.

6.5 Religious Ideology

It is indeed worth addressing religious ideology however, performing an extensive theological discourse is beyond the scope of the study. For the sake of clarity, the only work I will address with respect to religious ideology is what ISIS adhered to in specific relation to sexual violence.

---

[183] Barstow, Anne Llewellyn. "Introduction." *War's Dirty Secret: Rape, Prostitution, and Other Crimes against Women.* Ed. Anne Llewellyn. Barstow. Cleveland, OH: Pilgrim, 2000. 1-10. Print.

Here are ISIS's guidelines for the treatment of slaves as discussed in a pamphlet distributed by ISIS's Research and Fatwa Department:

Premise	Reference
Slavery frees women from *shirk* (disbelief) and causes conversions to Islam	"Ibn al-Jawzi said: 'Its meaning is that they were taken prisoner and put in bonds but when they got to know the truth of Islam they entered into it voluntarily so they entered Paradise, so the compulsion to imprisonment and bondage was the first cause' (Fath al-Bari 6/145)"
Slavery illustrates the supremacy of captors	"And for the girl of a spouse whom our arrows have given in marriage [i.e. for sex], it is permissible to consummate the marriage with her [i.e. lie carnally with her] even if she has not been divorced."
Punishment of *kuffar* (unbelievers)	"God Almighty has said: 'And the one whom God humiliates, there is no one to ennoble him' (al-Hajj 18) [Qur'an 22:18]."
Slavery is in the *Sunnah* (teachings of Prophet Mohammed)	"And also the Ahl al-Seer mentioned that the Prophet (SAWS) had four slave girls (concubines), and they were: Maria, and she was the mother of his son Ibrahim, Rayhana, a girl he acquired among some of the captives, and Jariya given to him as a gift by Zaynab bint Jahash."
Captivity and slavery are the	"This person made captive and

mercy of God	enslaved should be provided with residence, security, stability, food, and drink. And thus she should be able to escape from atrocities and vices, and living in the ways and canals of garbage."
Captivity increases offspring of mujahideen (fighters)	"There is no doubt that increasing numbers is strength for the Muslims, and the fact that the concubine slave girls may give birth is not an ugly or condemnable matter."
Slaves reward *mujahideen* (fighters)	"For men to be allowed to take women captive and purchase them, and this is something by which unmarried men benefit most or the one who desires multiple [spouses] but cannot be just, so for him is the possession of the right hand as wealth."[184]

This table summarized the tenets of religious ideology ISIS has used to justify sexual violence. It is clear from the references that most of the verses come from hadiths and not from the Koran, which essentially means that ISIS's use of sexual violence is highly subjective and merits further investigation from the perspective of religious ideology.

6.6 Summary

The three main theories were tested and it is clear that evolution theory does not entirely explain ISIS's sexual violence as the main motive for its use of sexual violence is not procreation. Feminist theory

---

[184] Malik, Nikita. *Trafficking Terror: How Modern Slavery and Sexual Violence Fund Terrorism*. Publication. London: Henry Jackson Society, 2017. Print.

does not entirely explain ISIS's use of sexual violence, as anonymity was certainly not the reason behind the use of sexual violence, and personal power scenarios did not play the largest role. Although strategic rape concept is the theory that resonated the most, it also fails to explain ISIS's use of sexual violence completely because the familiarity was also not a key reason. Although all three theories do not entirely explain sexual violence, it is worth addressing that along the way, the possibility why none of these theories "fit" is because ISIS's use of sexual violence should be understood from the religious ideology element, which needs separate research.

Chapter 7:
Conclusion

How can ISIS's use of sexual violence against the Yezidi women in Iraq since August 2014 be explained?

After extensive investigation, ISIS's use of sexual violence against the Yezidi women can best be explained by elements pertaining to all three theories under examination in this book: evolution theory, feminist theory, and strategic rape concept. What both feminist and strategic rape concept failed to account for, evolution theory was able to answer, such as the concept of proximate causation. For instance, proximate causation would imply that that ISIS's fighters, many of whom have been captured, should be examined into in order to understand what formed or caused their behaviors, as it could be genetics, psychology, or environment. This concept was left out by feminist theory and strategic rape concept. Feminist theory, on the other hand, emphasized context yet heavily relied on desexualizing the act of rape in war as rape appears to have been more violent than sexual. Strategic rape concept has the highest resonance with respect to this single case study, even though the act of rape is sexualized and there are indicators that the act also entails elements of violence. Furthermore, even though some victims were able to identify their rapists, other victims were not unable to do so. Yet, strategic rape was able to shed light on the strategic gains that resulted from ISIS's use of sexual violence such as the boost in morale, deterring the enemy, and securing a strategically important area. ISIS's sexual violence against Yezidi women is a multilayered topic that can best be explained by different theories as they all reveal part of the explanation.

7.1 Reflection

Conducting this research was very challenging for many reasons. It hits close to home to me as I have lost a family member to gender-based violence. I wished there were instances in which I was more objective and felt less guilty about asking survivors painful questions. More guidance on how to deal with secondary trauma would be of great help to future projects of this type.

On a less personal note, this research highlighted many possibilities to further the study of sexual violence. Testing the three main theories highlighted that, when combined, they can help explain sexual violence in the absence of a detailed and difficult to obtain understanding of religious discourse, and absent sufficient information to explore variations of sexual violence in greater detail. Elements from all three theories give a revealing picture, yet not the whole picture. Future research should focus on creating a framework consisting of multiple approaches and theories.

Works Cited

Barstow, Anne Llewellyn. "Introduction." *War's Dirty Secret: Rape, Prostitution, and Other Crimes against Women.* Ed. Anne Llewellyn. Barstow. Cleveland, OH: Pilgrim, 2000. 1-10. Print.

Barstow, Anne Llewellyn. "Rape as a Weapon of Armed Conflict." *War's Dirty Secret: Rape, Prostitution, and Other Crimes against Women.* Ed. Anne Llewellyn. Barstow. Cleveland, OH: Pilgrim, 2000. 45. Print.

Bernard, Vincent, Mariya Nikolova, Elvina Pothelet, and Jamie A. Williamson, eds. "Sexual Violence in Armed Conflict." *International Review of the Red Cross- Humanitarian Debate: Law, Police, Action* 96.894 (2014): 427-655. Print.

Boghani, Priyanka. "Where the Black Flag of ISIS Flies A Look at the Nine Countries Where the Terror Group Has Formal Affiliates." *Where the Black Flag of ISIS Flies.* PBS, 13 May 2016. Web. 25 May 2018.

Brownmiller, Susan. "The Mass Psychology of Rape: An Introduction." *Against Our Will: Men, Women and Rape.* New York: Ballantine, 1993. 11-15. Print.

Brownmiller, Susan. "Two Studies in American History." *Against Our Will: Men, Women and Rape.* New York: Ballantine, 1993. 140-73. Print.

Brownmiller, Susan. "War." *Against Our Will: Men, Women and Rape.* New York: Ballantine, 1993. 31-113. Print.

Butler, Judith. "Performative Acts and Gender Constitution: An Essay in Phenomenology and Feminist Theory." *Theatre Journal* 40.4 (1988): 519-31. *JSTOR [JSTOR].* Web. 4 Dec. 2017.

Cahill, Ann J. "Foucault, Rape, and the Construction of the Feminine Body." *Hypatia* 15.1 (2000): 43-63. *JSTOR [JSTOR]*. Web. 1 Mar. 2017.

Callimachi, Rukmini. "ISIS Enshrines a Theology of Rape." *The New York Times*. The New York Times, 13 Aug. 2015. Web. 4 Aug. 2018.   <https://www.nytimes.com/2015/08/14/world/middleeast/isis-enshrines-a-theology-of-rape.html>.

Carlson, Jennifer, and Raka Ray. "Feminist Theory." *Oxford Bibliographies*. Oxford, 20 Nov. 2011. Web. 04 Dec. 2017.

Fuccaro, Nelida. *Aspects of the Social and Political History of the Yazidi Enclave of Jabal Sinjar (Iraq) under the British Mandate, 1919-1932*. Thesis. Durham University, 1994. Durham: Durham Theses, 1994. Print.

Gerges, Fawaz A. "Acknowledgements." Preface. *ISIS: A History*. Princeton, NJ: Princeton UP, 2017. Xv-Xix. Print.

Gerges, Fawaz A. "Down the Rabbit Hole and into the History of ISIS." Introduction. *ISIS: A History*. Princeton, NJ: Princeton UP, 2017. 1-22. Print.

Gerges, Fawaz A. *ISIS: A History*. Princeton, NJ: Princeton UP, 2017. Print.

Gerges, Fawaz A. "The World According to ISIS." *ISIS: A History*. Princeton, NJ: Princeton UP, 2017. 23-49. Print.

Gottschall, Jonathan. "Explaining Wartime Rape." *The Journal of Sex Research* 41.2 (2004): 129-36. *JSTOR*. Web. 21 Apr. 2017.

Guest, John S. "The Yezidi Religion." *The Yezidis: A Study in Survival*. London: Routledge & Kegan Paul, Associated Book (UK)Ltd., 1987. 28-41. Print.

"Guidelines for Investigating Conflict-Related Sexual and Gender-based Violence Against Men and Boys." *Institute for International Criminal Investigations*. Institute for International Criminal Investigations, 29 Feb. 2016. Web. 05 Aug. 2018.

Hashim, Ahmed S. "Understanding the Islamic State." *The Caliphate at War: The Ideological, Organisational and Military Innovations of Islamic State*. London: Hurst, 2016. 3-16. Print.

Henderson, Holly. "Feminism, Foucault, and Rape: A Theory and Politics of Rape Prevention." *Berkeley Journal of Gender, Law & Justice* 22.1 (2007): 225-130. Web. 25 Mar. 2017.

Jalabi, Raya. "Who Are the Yazidis and Why Is Isis Hunting Them?" *The Guardian.* Guardian News and Media, 11 Aug. 2014. Web. 25 May 2018.

Khalaf, Farida, and Andrea C. Hoffmann. "The Catastrophe." *The Girl Who Beat ISIS.* London: Square PEG, 2017. 30-57. Print.

Malik, Nikita. *Trafficking Terror: How Modern Slavery and Sexual Violence Fund Terrorism.* Publication. London: Henry Jackson Society, 2017. Print.

Murad, Nadia, and Jenna Krajeski. "Chapter 5." *The Last Girl: My Story of Captivity, and My Fight against the Islamic State.* 1st ed. New York: Tim Duggan, 2017. 46-55. Print.

Murad, Nadia. "Chapter 1." *The Last Girl: My Story of Captivity, and My Fight against the Islamic State.* 1st ed. New York: Tim Duggan, 2017. 3-14. Print.

Murad, Nadia. "Chapter 3." *The Last Girl: My Story of Captivity, and My Fight against the Islamic State.* New York: Tim Duggan, 2017. 27-35. Print.

Murad, Nadia. "Chapter 4." *The Last Girl: My Story of Captivity, and My Fight against the Islamic State.* 1st ed. New York: Tim Duggan, 2017. 125-35. Print.

Neuman, W. Lawrence. "Field Research and Focus Group Research." *Social Research Methods:Qualitative and Quantitative Approaches: Pearson New International Edition.* Harlow: Pearson Education Limited, 2014. 431-76. Print.

Neuman, W. Lawrence. "Qualitative and Quantitative Sampling." *Social Research Methods:Qualitative and Quantitative Approaches: Pearson New International Edition.* Harlow: Pearson Education Limited, 2014. 246-80. Print.

Neuman, W. Lawrence. *Social Research Methods: Qualitative and Quantitative Appraoches*. 7th ed. Essex: Pearson Education Limited, 2014. Print.

Neuman, W. Lawrence. "What Are the Major Types of Social Research?" *Social Research Methods: Qualitative and Quantitative Approaches: Pearson New International Edition*. Harlow: Pearson Education Limited, 2014. 25-54. Print.

Office of the Special Representative of the Secretary-general on Sexual Violence in Conflict. *Report of the Secretary-General on Conflict-Related Sexual Violence*. Rep. no. 249. United Nations, 15 Apr. 2017. Web. 25 July 2018. <http://www.un.org/en/events/elimination-of-sexual-violence-in-conflict/pdf/1494280398.pdf>.

Persaud, Nadini. "Primary Data Source." *Encyclopedia of Research Design*. Ed. Neil J. Salkind. Thousand Oaks: SAGE Publications, 2012. 1095-097. Print.

Salzman, Todd. ""Rape Camps", Forced Impregnation, and Ethnic Cleansing." *War's Dirty Secret: Rape, Prostitution, and Other Crimes against Women*. Ed. Anne Llewellyn. Barstow. Cleveland, OH: Pilgrim, 2000. 63-92. Print.

Szyjka, Sebastian. "Understanding Research Paradigms:Trends in Science Education Research." *Problems of Education in the 21st Century* 43 (2012): 110-19. Print.

Than, Ker. "What Is Darwin's Theory of Evolution?" *LiveScience*. Purch, 13 May 2015. Web. 03 Dec. 2017.

Thornhill, Randy, and Craig Palmer. "The Social Explanation of Rape." *A Natural History of Rape: Biological Bases of Sexual Coercion*. Cambridge, MA: MIT, 2000. 123-52. Print.

Thornhill, Randy, and Craig T. Palmer. "Rape and Evolutionary Theory." *A Natural History of Rape: Biological Bases of Sexual Coercion*. Cambridge, MA: MIT, 2000. 1-30. Print.

Thornhill, Randy, and Craig T. Palmer. "Why Do Men Rape?" *A Natural History of Rape: Biological Bases of Sexual Coercion*. Cambridge, MA: MIT, 2000. 53-84. Print.

Townsend, Mark. "Rape and Slavery Was Lure for UK Isis Recruits with History of Sexual Violence." *The Guardian*. Guardian News and Media, 07 Oct. 2017. Web. 05 Aug. 2018.

Wood, Elisabeth Jean. "Conflict-related Sexual Violence and the Policy Implications of Recent Research." *International Review of the Red Cross* 96.894 (2014): 457-78. *JSTOR [JSTOR]*. Web. 2 Apr. 2017.

Wood, Elisabeth Jean. "Multiple Perpetrator Rape during War." *Multiple Perpetrator Rape during War." Handbook on the Study of Multiple Perpetrator Rape: A Multidisciplinary Response to an International Problem*. Ed. Miranda A.H Horvath and Jessica Woodhams. London: Routledge, Taylor & Francis, 2013. 132-59. Print.

Wood, Elisabeth Jean. "Variation in Sexual Violence during War." *Politics & Society* 34.3 (2006): 307-41. *Politics & Society*. Sage Publications, Sept. 2006. Web. 25 Mar. 2017.

Yin, Robert K. *Case Study Research and Applications: Design and Methods*. 6th ed. Thousand Oaks, CA: SAGE Publications, 2018. Print.

Yin, Robert K. "Collecting Case Study Evidence- The Principles You Should Follow in Working With Six Sources of Evidence." *Case Study Research and Applications: Design and Methods*. 6th ed. Los Angeles: SAGE, 2018. 110-63. Print.

Yin, Robert K. "Designing Case Studies Identifying Your Case(s) and Establishing the Logic of Your Case Study." *Case Study Research and Applications: Design and Methods*. 6th ed. Los Angeles, CA: SAGE, 2018. 24-80. Print.